My Golden Wave

Mee Sook Lee

My Golden Wave
Mee Sook Lee

All rights reserved. No parts
of this book should be reproduced,
photocopied electronically,
or recorded without the permission
of the copyright holder.

Copyright © Mee Sook Lee,
December 2020

ISBN: 9798586643131
Imprint: Independently published

Published by
The Hyung S. Lee Family
Chicago

Dedication

To my dear parents: Hyun Jae Kim and Choi Soon Kim, my husband Hyung Sub Lee, and my sons: Joseph M. Lee and Justin M. Lee.

Contents

Dedication..3

Acknowledgements..6

My Humble Beginnings..8

My Parents' Migration
to South Korea...12

Kimchi...16

My Husband's Family Migrates
to South Korea...22

How My Parents Met...26

Some Korean Social Customs................................34

Ancestral Rites..38

Religion...45

The Arts...50

Korean Language..52

My Precious Family..55

My Father's Endurance...59

A Big Set-Back...64

Primary and High School Education....................67

Going to College..70

My Friends in College...74

Effort to Build My Career....................................78

Marriage...80

Arriving in the U.S.A..86

Pregnant with My First Child............................90

How My Family Survived
in America with Little..96

Losing One of My Babies..................................99

Becoming Pro-Life..102

Teaching Catechism..106

Visiting My Mother...110

My Brother Jong Sun 114

Closing Ravenswood...120

To Holy Family Hospital..................................124

My Son Joseph..131

My Son Justine..139

My Brother Jong Hwa......................................144

The Last Days of My Father............................151

Taking My Sister Out
of a Mental Institution......................................154

My Health Scare...165

Messages from Friends: A Kind Loyal Friend
by Claudia Kowal..171

Meeting Mee Sook Lee
by Sr. Stella 174

5

Acknowledgements

I am very thankful to God who created me and placed me on this beautiful earth and helped me to profess my love to my Lord and Saviour through Baptism in 1973.

To my parents, Hyun Jae Kim, and Choi Soon Kim, I say: rest in peace until we meet again in Heaven.

I will always be grateful for the gift of my husband, Hyung S. Lee with whom I have shared the past forty-four years of my life. Thank you for encouraging me to share my story in a book. Your persistence in asking when the book was coming up helped me to take my first baby steps toward writing my story.

I can't thank God enough for my two wonderful sons and my daughters-in-law, for letting me be their mother: Joseph and Justin Lee, Jin Sook and Jane and my grandchildren: Lauren and Henry, you are precious to me.

My brothers, Jong Sun (46) and Jong Wha (51) in Heaven. I remember you always. Rest in Peace.

My beloved sister Hee Sook Kim, now in a long-term care hospital in South Korea: I am happy God gave me the strength to work hard and get you out of the mental institute where you had been confined for thirty years. You are always in my heart.

I am thankful to God for my nephews Min Woo and Hyun Woo.

I am indebted to my father-in-law, Sun Yoo Lee (R.I.P) and my mother-in-law, Soon Duck Lee (R.I.P) who for many years treated me as their own daughter. I came to the U.S.A with no family; they were always there, loving and caring about me.

My brother-in-law, Chi Sup Lee, and my sisters-in-law, In Ok Yang and Choon Ja Chi and Leanne Choi, who was also my college classmate (through whom I got to know my husband), I thank you all for being family to me. I would not have made it this far without your love and caring hearts.

I am also very thankful to Sister Stella's love and encouragement. She too like my husband, has been asking me to put my story in a book so my children, grandchildren, friends, and everyone who might read it may know where I came from and learn from my life experiences.

I ask God to bless all the relatives and friends I have ever crossed path with, and who have spiced my life with joy and miracles. I have not mentioned each one of you by name because I fear to leave any of you out as my memory is deteriorating.

My Humble Beginnings

My Golden Wave

I am a beloved daughter of Hyun Jae Kim and Choi Soon Kim (R.I.P).

In Korea people of the same last name are not allowed to marry each other. They are believed to have originated from the same family lineage or clan. But my parents (both Kims) married because they came from different clans in Korea.

My roots are from what is now known as North Korea. My grandfather on my father's side was a landlord who had tenants. He lived well in the middle class before he lost everything during the era of the communist rule.

In August 1945, the Soviet Union and the United States divided Korea. The Soviet Union occupied the Northern Part of Korea and the United States occupied the Southern Part, divided by 38th Parallel as indicated on the map on page 11.

Under Communist Rule, the conditions of life in the North deteriorated so much and people suffered a lot. Many lost their property and were hungry and unable to work or afford a place to stay.

With very cold winters, many people were left with no choice except to move south where the conditions were not so bitter. My father was among those who were forced to migrate to what is now known as South Korea.

Negotiations between the two occupants failed during the Cold War and the Soviet Union failed to unify Korea. Therefore, elections were held only in the United States occupied South, while in the North, a leader was just appointed.

That led to the establishment of the Republic of Korea in the South which was promptly followed by the establishment of the Democratic People's Republic in North Korea.

The United States supported the South and the Soviet Union supported the North. Each government claimed sovereignty over the whole Korean Peninsula.

In 1950, after years of hostilities, North Korea invaded South Korea in attempt to unify the Peninsula under its communist rule. That led to the Korean War, which lasted from 1950 to 1953, and left the two Koreas completely separated to this day.

My Golden Wave

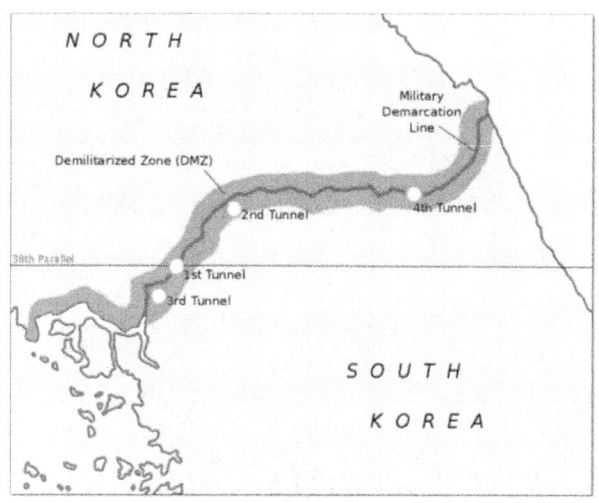

The Divided Korea

My Parents' Migration to South Korea

My Golden Wave

My father moved from Park Chun near Pyongyang in North Korea to Seoul in South Korea for further education.

When the Soviet Union took over North Korea, all rich people's assets and land were confiscated. Children of tenants (proletarian level) could go to school, but bourgeoise's children were not allowed to go to school. They had to work in factories and farms.

My father said that even though he had to work on a farm with bare feet, what hurt him the most was not to go to school. His father was not happy when my father and his brothers decided to leave home to go to South Korea to study. In South Korea dreams could be pursued through education and hard work.

Later, my father tried to enlist in the army, but was not accepted because he had a flat foot. He ended up serving as a police officer.

My father's older brother was kidnapped and taken back to North Korea. And his middle brother enrolled in College at Seoul University, but was shot and killed by unknown people.

At that point, my father had no immediate family at all, until he met my mother, and they created a new family.

My mother was from Ham Heung in North Korea. She migrated to the South after the Korean War (1.4 Retreat) with the United Forces Army.

It happened so fast, one day, my mother, then a young working girl undergoing Military Training, returned home from work and found her house bombed down and her -

My Golden Wave

parents nowhere to be found. She became an orphan with no close relative at all.

As many other refugees and orphans were retreating to the North, she joined the trail. That is where she encountered the United Forces Army, and like everybody else, surrendered to survive.

When the army went South to Seoul, she followed because she was now one of the helpers in the United Forces Army, as she had an Army training and some experience.

When the Army arrived in Seoul, the city was empty; the people had moved further south to escape the war. But there was a lot of Korean winter food (kimchi) and rice. As kimchi is stored outside in the ground in pots during wintertime, the migrating Army was able to get it easily and survive hunger.

My Golden Wave

The United Forces Army went South to Seoul

Kimchi

Kimchi is fermented vegetable food that is served as basic and essential part of every Korean meal. Napa cabbage sustains fermentation for a long period of time. With rice and kimchi many people survived hunger during the Korean War.

Kimchi Napa Cabbage used to make Kimchi

My Golden Wave

prepared Kimchi cabbage used to make Kimchi

My Golden Wave

Stored Kimchi in a pot under the ground

My Golden Wave

Kimchi pots, also used to keep soy sauce, soybean paste, red pepper paste.

My Golden Wave

Kimchi pots stored outside during winter

My Golden Wave

My mother taught me so much about Korean food because it is an important part of our cultural identity. Traditional Korean food is mainly grain, especially rice and fresh vegetables. A Korean meal consists of rice, soup and many side dishes including kimchi. There are more than 160 varieties of kimchi. The most favorable type is the spicy *paech'u* known as Chinese Cabbage Kimchi. In autumn, families in *kimjang* devoted several days to preparing the winter supply of Kimchi.

Many families today buy their Kimchi in supermarkets, but there are some that still make their own like my mother used to.

Other popular Korean dishes are *bibimbap* (rice mixed with vegetables, egg, a spicy sauce, and sometimes meat), *pulgogi* or *bulgogi* (marinated meat grilled over charcoal), *samgyet'ang* (a soup of stewed whole chicken stuffed with rice and ginseng), this one is eaten as healing, particularly during hot weather.

Koreans have hundreds of ways to mix vegetables and wild greens for long storage, and they also treasure raw fish.

My Husband's Family Migration to South Korea

My Golden Wave

In Spring 1947, my father-in-law, Sun You Lee and my mother-in-law Soon Duck Hong decided to move to South Korea.

When my father-in-law lost his job as Japanese floor mattress maker in North Korea, it became hard for him to support his family of seven. That is, with his wife and five children: In Ok (11), Chi Sup (10), Woo Sup (8), Choon Ja (3) and Hyung Sub (1). Therefore, my father-in-law and mother-in-law decided to go to Seoul where my mother-in-law had relatives.

When my mother-in-law asked my father in law's family to go to South Korea, they refused. They asked whether they were going to give them free meals in the south.

Early in the morning on the day my father-in-law's family moved to South Korea, my mother-in-law packed rice (*joo muk bab*) and some family belongings. My father-in-law carried the beddings and Choon Ja (who was three years old) sitting on top of the beddings. My mother-in-law carried the one-year-old baby (now my husband) on her back and some belongings on her head, and they walked to the train station.

They took a train to Chul Won where the railroad had been cut by North Korea; trains could not go beyond that city.

Trains from the North were always full, as many people were trying to move to South Korea. They even sat on top.

When the family got off the train at Chul Won, they walked a dangerous cliff; below was the Han Tan River. -

My Golden Wave

Woo Sup almost fell off the cliff but was helped by a young couple that was also on the trail.

When they reached at the 38th Parallel border, security checked all their things. They took all their photos and their important belongings including jewelry. Fortunately, they let them proceed on to South Korea.

My sister-in-law remembers her family walking up and down the cliffs at night, hearing insects and getting scared. Even now when she hears those insects she is reminded of that horrible time.

In some places they had to pay a guide to lead them, for they did not know which direction to go.

While on their journey, they came across a stream of water and a small village. That is where they rinsed the rice they had carried and made a meal. It was their first meal in South Korea.

After they rested, they took a train to Seoul Station. From Seoul Station they walked to the refugee camp which was known as Jang Choon Dong Park.

At the camp they were served boiled wheat. It was not delicious, but it was better than going hungry. At that point, my mother-in-law remembered her North Korean family that had stayed behind.

So, when she met her cousin at the refugee camp, she asked him to go back to North Korea with a letter she wrote asking them to come down to South Korea too, as there were free meals.

My Golden Wave

Her cousin went back with the letter and my mother-in-law's family migrated to South Korea. But her husband's side refused to move to South Korea.

After some time, my father-in-law found a job as a security guard in a factory. The Company provided him with one big room for his family to stay in.

The children started school. It was an exceedingly difficult time, but as if that were not enough the Korean War started in 1950 and schools closed. Only Chi Sup, the older boy was able to graduate from Dang San Primary School while living at the place of their first settlement.

Chang Sup and Kyung Ok were born in South Korea. Unfortunately, Woo Sup and Chang Sup lost their lives during the war. I remember them always in my daily prayer for the deceased. Their precious short lives are not forgotten.

The end of the rail from North to South Korea

How My Parents Met

My Golden Wave

My mother was introduced to my father by some people who happened to know them both, and they later married.

My father and mother

My Golden Wave

I was the first-born child of my parents. They were overjoyed, especially my father, because he knew he would survive through me. I was very precious to him. He took me everywhere: to collect mineral mountain water, to the market and even to the bathing places where only men were allowed.

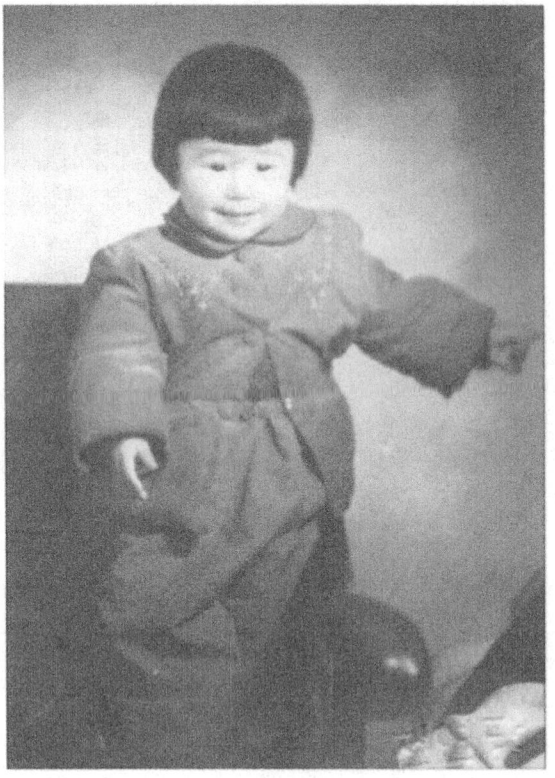

My first Birthday

My Golden Wave

My father and me

My Golden Wave

Me at age four

My Golden Wave

Me and my friends

My Golden Wave

I am happy I brought joy to my father. It is hard to imagine the feeling of being alone, not knowing whether you will ever have a close relative. And not knowing whether your parents and relatives are dead or still alive.

My father died without finding any of his immediate family members. His wife and children were his consolation.

A few years after my mother arrived in South Korea, she was told that her brother was still alive, and that he was in South Korea too. More than thirty years later when she finally would have found him, he died. Fortunately, she found her sister-in law and nephew and niece. That is how far my mother's side goes.

My parents lived a simple life on a police officer's income, which was not much at that time.

My mother cut her own hair with a razor blade and combed it nicely because she could not afford going to a hairdresser. Nobody could tell she never went to have her hair done because she was so good at doing it herself. I think she would have gotten a lot of money as a hairdresser if she had opened a shop.

Mama was a real home maker who could not lose a penny. She used to make sellers cut radish to make sure it was good before she bought it. If she bought slippers and one or both broke before twenty-four hours, she returned the pair to the store to exchange it. She said that if it broke in such a short period of time, it was not well made.

If the seller refused to exchange the sleepers, Mama sat at the store until the seller agreed to give her a new pair. Anything with a defect, she could not buy. People called her someone from "Tto Soon Yi." People like that work extremely hard and cannot afford to lose anything.

My Golden Wave

But even though my mother was like that, when someone came to our home hungry or in need, she never let that person go away hungry or empty handed. I learned a lot from her generosity.

My Mother

Some Korean Social Customs

My Golden Wave

Before I proceed with my personal story; I would like to talk about some Korean social customs in which my life is rooted.

My parents taught me that respect for ancestors, age, and seniority is important in a Korean family, work, and social life. Age and marital status determine seniority in the community and influences relations.

Rites of passage involve rituals marking life-cycle milestones and the observation of holidays. For example, a baby's first one hundred days, marriage and the sixty-first birthday.

A child's one hundred days were celebrated because many children used to die within the first one hundred days from whooping cough or measles. If a child made it through those first one hundred days, there was reason to celebrate and hope for him or her to live. The tradition stayed even after vaccines were discovered to prevent those diseases.

The sixty-first birthday was a big milestone for people to celebrate, for not many were living that long. This tradition is also still alive today.

My Golden Wave

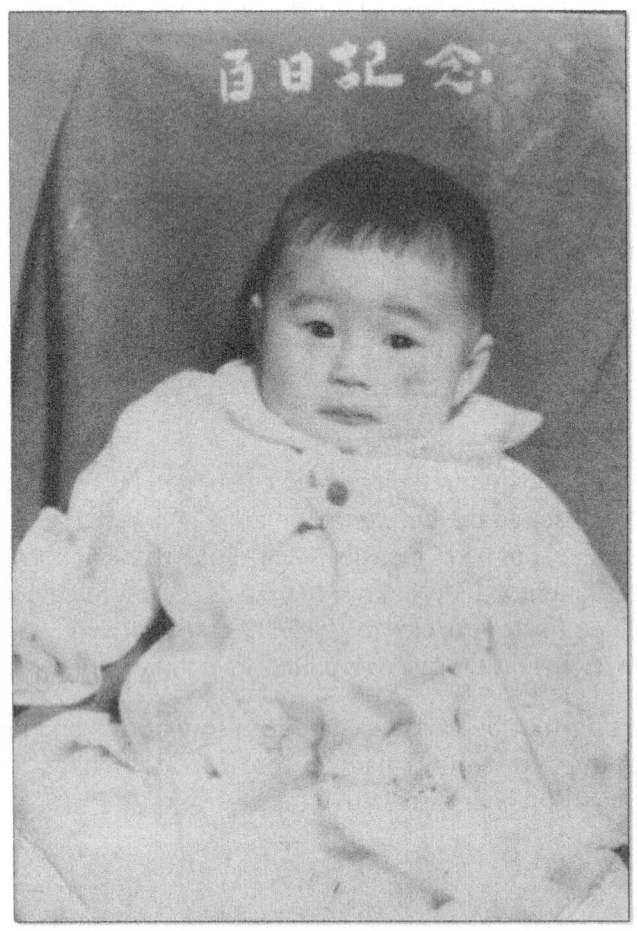

My first one hundred days on earth

My Golden Wave

My brother's first one hundred days on earth

Ancestral Rites

My Golden Wave

According to traditional Korean belief, the spirit of a departed family member does not leave the earth for several generations; thus, deceased parents and grandparents are still considered part of the family.

Ancestral rites are performed to honor the dead on their death anniversaries and on major holidays like the *Sŏllal* (Lunar New Year) and *Chusŏk* (Harvest Moon Festival) known as Korean Thanksgiving, observed according to the Lunar Calendar.

My in-laws grave

Honoring my in-laws

On those holidays, families gather in the ancestral hometown or at the home of the head of the family. The celebration includes the formal, respectful greeting of elders, eating of special foods such as specific types of rice cakes *(ddŏk),* and the wearing of traditional dress (hanbok).

Hanbok was the traditional dress before the influence of the West. But some Koreans still wear it especially for weddings, family meetings, holidays, and funerals. Women and girls' formal *hanbok* consist of several layers of undergarments under a colorful, long billowing skirt and a short jacket closed with a long tie.

My Golden Wave

Women and girls' *hanbok*

My Golden Wave

The men's and boys' *hanbok* consist of full-legged pants and a long, wide-sleeved jacket. There are different *hanbok* for special occasions, such as weddings, babies' birthdays, and the sixty-first birthday celebrations.

Men and boy's *hanbok*

My Golden Wave

Colors of dresses in Korea had different meanings rising from history. *Obangsaek* is the traditional Korean color spectrum, made up of black, white, red, yellow, and blue. *Ogansaek* is the other spectrum that comes from mixing the primary colors, such as green, light blue, bright red, sulfur yellow and violet. Below are how colors were interpreted in Korea:

Red represented passion and love, good fortune, and wealth. It was common for women to wear it for their wedding. It also represented masculine energy. Today people use it for sports as it is believed to bring strength.

Black was the color of infinity, creation, intelligence, and wisdom. It was mainly worn by intellectuals. It was the color of darkness and death as well.

Blue used to be worn by women of the court for their skirts and the coat of court officials, it was also the color of a new birth, brightness, and clarity.

Yellow used to be worn by royals only, and gold by emperors. It represented the center of the universe and was associated with the Earth. Sometimes unmarried girls wore light yellow color to show their maidenhood.

Green had the same meaning as blue. It represented a fresh start, youth, and young energy, but was often worn by married women.

White, represented metal. It was the color of purity and modesty, life, truth, peace, and patriotism.

My Golden Wave

Today people pay little attention to those color interpretations of the dresses. They just make what attracts their eye. The world has changed.

Religion

My Golden Wave

I would also like to talk about religion because it is an integral part of Korean Culture. Koreans from time immemorial acknowledged that there was a Supreme Being.

There were many religious practices in Korea to honor the Creator: Buddhism, Confucianism, Daoism, Shamanism, and Christianity which was introduced in the late 18th century.

Unlike other parts of the world, Christianity was introduced in Korea by lay people. It has gone through a lot of persecution. People gave their lives for the Church to take sprout in South Korea. The Catholic Church has so far canonized 103 martyrs in Korea. Those martyrs became the strength of the Church. Even though it is less than a century old, it is strong in faith.

Below is an excerpt from *All Saints and Martyrs* website that gives more information in a summarized narrative of how the Korean martyrs decided to give their lives for the faith.

> The group was headed by Paul Yun Ji-Chung, a nobleman who converted to Catholicism and refused to have his deceased mother buried under the traditional Confucian rite. His refusal led to a massive persecution of Christians called the Sinhae Persecution in 1791. Paul was beheaded on December 8, 1791, together with his cousin, James Kwon Sang-yeon.
>
> They were the first members of the Korean nobility to be killed for the faith. Among the –

martyrs in this group are Fr. James Zhou Wen-mo (1752-1801), a Chinese priest who secretly ministered to the Christians in Korea; Augustine Jeong Yak-Jong (1760-1801), the husband of St. Cecilia Yu So-sa and father of Sts. Paul Chong Ha-sang and Elizabeth Chong Chong-hye; Columba Kang Wan-suk (1761-1801), known as the "catechist of the Korean Martyrs"; Augustine Yu Hang-geom (1756-1801), also known as the "apostle of Jeolla-do"; and Maria Yi Seong-rye (1801-1840), the wife of St. Francis Choe Kyeong-hwan. Also included in the group are Augustine Yu Hang-geom's son John Yu Jeong-cheol (1779-1801) and his wife Lutgarda Yi Sun-i (1782-1802).

They both decided to live celibate lives to fully dedicate themselves to God, but the Confucian society, which greatly valued furthering the family line, made it impossible for them to live as celibates. Fr. James Zhou introduced the two to each other and suggested them to marry each other and live as a "virgin couple." The two were married in 1797 and were martyred 4 years later.

Many people from all over the world visit the Korean Martyrs Museum-Shrine in Jeoldusan where most of the Korean martyrs died from 1866 to 1873.

Like in the other parts of the world where missionaries lacked the knowledge of the cultures of the people, Korean converts were told to throw away most of their worship traditions to take on the new traditions of the evangelizers. A few traditions that survived and still survive today have been Christianized.

The honoring of the ancestors I talked about before, is one of those traditions that have been Christianized. When you compare it to the honoring of the saints in the Church, it was not different.

We honored our ancestors because it is from them God shaped our existence. And it is because of their courage to live under all circumstances that we continue the journey of life.

My Golden Wave

My parents belonged to no organized religion until later in life, but they believed God existed. In their hearts they knew God wanted every human being to be happy because every human being was created by God and is precious. That is why they extended their acts of kindness to all people they crossed paths with.

As I will narrate later, I was the first in my family to be baptized and to belong to a church, the Catholic Church.

The Arts

My Golden Wave

The other topic I feel I cannot leave out, is the Arts because they give identity to the Korean people.

South Korea is a country so rich in Creative Art; many products are decorated with imaginative designs and colors. For example, pottery, metalwork, and woodwork are always beautifully decorated to uplift the spirits of those who see them. What people drew or painted since time immemorial had a lot to say about the culture of the Korean people.

Most of Korean Art can now be found in Museums like the National Museum, *Gyeongbokgung* Palace, Seoul Museum of History and many others. If you happen to visit Korea, do not miss visiting some of those museums to learn more about the Korean Culture.

For the Performing Arts, there were traveling troupes that performed puppet plays, did acrobatics, jugglers and dancers in Korean villages and towns. One of the oldest performances of Korean Dance and Theatre is the Masked Dance.

Villagers in different areas of the country formed folk groups and performed their own local versions of the masked dances.

Today you can still see the Masked Dance in *Kyŏnggi* and South *Kyŏngsang* provinces as well as in parts of North Korea. Performers of that dance are men.

Masks are made from paper or gourds and sometimes from wood. They are boldly painted to represent the characters.

The Korean Language

My Golden Wave

Language is an integral part of the Korean Culture. The main language in Korea is called Korean. Some people say it originated from the Altaic family of languages in northern Asia which includes the Mongol, Turkic, Finnish, Hungarian, and Tungusic (Manchu) languages.

Korean Language has a rich history which dates to Silla Kingdom. China influenced Korean a lot during that time. For centuries, Koreans used Chinese characters to write their language, but in the 15th century a new alphabet, known today as *Hangeul*, was developed by Sejong the Great, the 4th King of Joseon dynasty

The Korean Language has evolved greatly since the division of Korea into North and South, with political influence, instead of the natural evolving that happens to languages as the world changes. Korean of the North and South has started to drift apart, even though the foundation is still the same.

Despite all that, Korean is one of the major languages of the world spoken by more than 80 million people.

My Golden Wave

The Korean Alphabet

CONSONANTS						
ㄱ	ㄴ	ㄷ	ㄹ	ㅁ	ㅂ	ㅅ
G/K	N	D/T	R/L	M	B/P	S
ㅇ	ㅈ	ㅊ	ㅋ	ㅌ	ㅍ	ㅎ
NG	J	CH	K	T	P	H

VOWELS						
ㅏ	ㅐ	ㅑ	ㅒ	ㅓ	ㅔ	ㅕ
A	AE	YA	YAE	EO	E	YEO
ㅖ	ㅗ	ㅘ	ㅙ	ㅚ	ㅛ	ㅜ
YE	O	WA	WAE	OE	YO	U
ㅝ	ㅞ	ㅟ	ㅠ	ㅡ	ㅢ	ㅣ
WO	WE	WI	YU	EU	UI	I

54

My Precious Family

My Golden Wave

My parents went through some tough decisions about the growing number of their family. It grew and included my two brothers and sister.

After two children, me and my brother, Jong Sun, my parents felt overwhelmed. And when my mother got pregnant with my brother Jong Hwa, she thought of abortion. But my father said they should keep the baby because it could be a boy.

Yes, it was a boy. Boys were more preferred and loved in the Korean Culture.

Again, when my mother got pregnant with her fourth child, she seriously thought of aborting the baby because life was hard already with the three of us. Still my father thought it could be a boy, but it was a girl.

Just because of having been born a girl at a wrong time, my sister went through what I call neglect and deprivation of love as a child. She was traumatized. She went as far as high school and her childhood trauma caught up with her. She did not go to College, she started roaming the streets and was hospitalized from time to time because of mental illness.

My mother decided to take my sister to a prayer place which was ran by a Protestant Minister. She thought she could be helped there. That place was later turned into a mental institution. She was institutionalized for thirty years there until when I took her out in 2013 after my father died that same year.

I refer to that as one of the biggest achievements of my life with the help of God. I felt it was my responsibility to help my sister get her life back.

My Golden Wave

Even though she is still struggling, being free is better than being institutionalized for life.

From left, Hee Sook (my baby sister), me, Jong Hwa (my 2nd brother) Jong Sun (my 1st brother)

My sister Hee Sook Kim

My Golden Wave

As a young girl, being the first born, I had a lot of responsibility to help my mother: laundry, babysitting, cleaning the house, and other chores except cooking. I had to help because my mother had her hands full and needed all the help she could get.

Despite a lot of chores, I am happy I still got a chance to play as a child and read my favorite books. We had no library in the village. We used to borrow books from the Principal's Office and return them the next day. So, if you wanted to finish the story you had to read fast. My favorite book was Three Kingdoms (Sam Kuk Ji).

Part of my precious family today, picture taken at Jane & Justin's wedding.

My Father's Endurance

My Golden Wave

My father said that the trials he went through while migrating from North Korea and living by himself, trying to begin a new life in South Korea, helped him to endure many hardships throughout his life. From a landlord's son to a poor boy (when North Korea became a Communist country), he taught himself to work hard.

In 1982 when my husband asked my father how to make money and be successful, my father wrote a letter of advice telling him to be responsible, plan well, save the money little by little, invest well, and diligently work hard. And, to remember to take care of his parents and relatives.

When I returned to South Korea for the first time to attend my brother's wedding, I was happy to bring back that letter to my husband. At his request, even though the writing and the paper have deteriorated, I am glad to include that letter in this book to keep my father's memory, greatly honored by my husband.

My Golden Wave

My father's letter to my husband- page 1

My Golden Wave

가 되었다.
동서로 취함은 알아 가지고 그라고 하였다에
서 사정인가 동서는 하분이 따르되었이
아니야 또는 훈련은 철저히 하고 計劃
은 세워 두 조금씩이라도 저축은 하며 돈은
쓸고 분수한 행동은 하며 돈은 키워라
그리고 고고한 행각은 하자 兄弟는
다른 사람 (부모 처자 가족 친척포함) 접촉 하기
는 원하는 사람이 되어도록 노력 하는 동시
交際할때는 물가서 해라 사람 곳으는
혀한는 도 효도는 깨고 분은 일어지
않은 사람은 죽은 사람이라고 생각 생각
하여 분들은 사람은 가리금 두어라
그리고 늙은 父에 잘보시지
1982. 5. 20
丈 人 書

My father's letter to my husband-page 2

My Golden Wave

My father knew nothing would come free to him. He therefore worked hard and even harder when he became a family man. But that struggle and stress most times took a toll on him and his family.

As a police officer, he worked many hours trying to enforce the law. He was very faithful and kept his dignity all the way. He never accepted bribes; that was hard for many police officers of that time, as they were not being paid enough and with families to support. Taking something from law breakers and letting them go free was the practice of the day. My father refused to do that.

Unfortunately, when he came home it was like an extension of his work. He got angry easily with my mother. That saddened me so much.

My mother used to ask him why he treated his family like criminals, but he could not answer that question. He failed to control himself due to the stress he was going through every day.

To make ends meet, my father tried to buy old houses, renovate them, and sell them. He did not sell many though; when he saw poor families with no place to live and could not afford to pay rent, he let them live in his renovated houses for free.

The only money that came in was when he rented some of his renovated houses to the American soldiers from the former nearby Army Station at Miari.

A Big Set-Back

My Golden Wave

One day, as my father was renovating one of his old houses, a big piece of wood fell on him and injured his back. He spent six months in hospital. We stayed with a neighbor as my mother took care of him.

Those were very dark times for my family because my father was the only source of income. Fortunately, those were still the golden days when everybody knew her or his neighbors and loved them like family. There is no way my mother would have been able to handle everything by herself if our neighbor, Seung Hoon's, mother did not step in to help. I am forever grateful to her.

When he was discharged from hospital, my father recuperated slowly at home. It was a big setback to the family, but it was a miracle the piece of wood did not hit any major nerves; he was able to walk and work again.

During the time when my father could not work, God sustained my family miraculously. One day, my mother found $20 on the street (it was a lot of money then). She used that money to apply wallpaper and doing the floor of one of the houses and then rented it out and supported us.

My Golden Wave

One of the houses my father renovated

Primary and High School Education

My Golden Wave

In 1960, at age seven, I started school at Shung In, a former Army Station that had been turned into a primary school. I was happy to go to school because I knew education would open doors for me.

One of my primary school teachers I remember the most is Miss Joeng Jong Lee. If you failed a test, she asked you to open both your hands and get a stroke. The number of mistakes you made determined the number of strokes you got.

One of my friends used to be very scared of Miss Lee. She would keep taking her hands away, and the more she did that, the more Miss Lee multiplied the strokes for her.

One day, one of the students hid Miss Lee's stick. But Miss Lee had a dream about where the stick had been hidden and she found it. When I remember that I laugh so hard.

At school, I quickly became famous because of my name, Mee Sook which means beautiful, but sounds like a Korean powdered food (Mi Sook Ga-Ru). From that, everybody knew me by face and by name.

The school building was not the best though, it was old and did not have good heating; it was uncomfortable.

I appreciated my mother very much; she was always home when I returned from school. When I called: "Mama, I am home," She welcomed me and listened to my stories from school. I felt she cared about me.

My father had suggested that my mother finds a job to increase the family earning, but she refused a paid job, to do what she regarded as the most important job, taking care of her children.

My Golden Wave

I graduated from primary school in 1966 and joined middle school for three years, and later, proceeded on to high school for three years.

The buildings in the middle and high schools were good with comfortable heating systems that made learning easy.

My school was now further from home, I had to take a bus to be on time. As most later buses were always very full, I used to sleep with my basic clothes on, so that in the morning, I could only wash my face, put school uniform on, eat breakfast and get on the first bus to school.

Every day I was the first to enter the school building. Sometimes I got there even before the door opened.

After school, I hardly stopped anywhere, not even at any bakery for a snack. I went straight home to help my mother with chores and to do my homework.

Going to College

My Golden Wave

My father wanted me to become a teacher because he thought it was a more decent job for a woman, but I failed the exam to enter a teacher training college.

My father then suggested that I go to a nursing school and earn a license to support my future family. I was not prepared for nursing at all, and science subjects were not my favorite.

For the entry exam, a friend helped me to memorize some Physics, Chemistry, and Biology to pass. I studied hard and passed both the written and the oral.

My oral interview was the most interesting; the examiner set a trick to test my interaction skills, I think. She set the chair I was supposed to sit on far away from her, by the door, instead of close to her. She wanted to find out what I would do when I entered the room.

When I entered the room, I realized something was weird. I had no clue it was part of the exam. I just did what maybe anyone who wanted to talk to someone would do. I lifted the chair and took it closer to her and sat down.

Later, when I learned it was part of the exam, I said, "Whew! Thank you, God!

Passing the entry exam got me into the Catholic Nursing College (1972) located at Kyung Woon Dong in Seoul.

The biggest miracle that happened to me in College was learning about Jesus Christ and receiving Baptism.

During my Catechism period, I went for a retreat with my Catholic schoolmates. That was the first retreat of my life.

My Golden Wave

The retreat house was near a beach surrounded with beautiful trees.

I was not an early riser, but for some reason, during that time I woke up early every morning. One morning, as I was walking through the woods back to the retreat house, it struck me; I started to realize that God created me and placed me in this beautiful world. All I had to do was to thank and praise Him. I cried all day for having lived without realizing that fact until then. After that I became a new person who understood that everything is a gift from God and precious. I started to look at life differently.

I was baptized in the Catholic Church on the 11th of February 1973.

With my classmates and the congregation
on my Baptism Day

My Golden Wave

After Baptism I was asked to go back to my hometown parish and register. At that time, there were very few catechists, so, my hometown Church asked me to teach Catechism to the children.

Two years after my Baptism, I was confirmed at Myung Dong Catholic Cathedral. I was overjoyed.

During the Confirmation Mass, I had no money to put in the offertory basket to show my appreciation. So, I made a quick decision to offer one of the two 18 caret gold rings my mother had given me. When the collection basket came around, I put it in. I offered something that I regarded as precious to me to express my love to Christ.

Life was changing fast, not only for me, but for my mother too. Now instead of being with her in the house and helping with many chores most of the time, I only had time to go back on weekends to help her with laundry.

My Friends in College

My Golden Wave

I had three special friends in College who made my life joyful despite all the school hustles. The four of us used to sing together harmonizing different songs and talking a lot about life.

We also supported each other in different ways. When I had a part time job of teaching my neighbor's children, I gave it to K.S., one of my friends, so she could earn some pocket money.

K.S. was going through a hard time, but I did not know she had more problems than she shared with me or with the three of us.

One day, in 1974, we (my friends and I) were shocked to wake up to the news that K.S. had taken her life by inhaling carbon monoxide from charcoal at home.

I cried and carried that sadness for a long time. I had put so much energy into helping her so that we could succeed together. I had introduced her to every friend I had including the priest and nun at our school even though she was not Catholic.

For my friend to make such a decision was hard for me to grasp. But now I understand; she might have had more problems in her family than she could handle or share at that time. I do not blame her anymore. I pray she rests in peace until we meet again.

K.S. had an older brother who had been injured in a car accident in high school (we learned about him after K.S.'s death). All her father's attention was on her brother. I think, though not sure, that might have been one of the reasons she took her life.

My Golden Wave

After K.S.'s death the three of us remained connected to her brother as she had been our close friend. We thought her brother needed support to recover from the shock. Unfortunately, the brother thought maybe I would fall for him, as I was the only one among the three who did not have a boyfriend.

One day, he got a wild idea to try me. He called my mother and asked for permission for me to go with him to visit K.S.'s grave. When my mother said yes, he hired a taxi to get us there.

The trip turned out with twists and turns. I had not gone to K.S.'s funeral; no one went for the funeral because the police were still investing the case. So, I did not know where her grave was.

We drove extremely far through back roads and I started to feel uneasy. He insisted that we continue driving and we would eventually find the graveyard where his sister was buried.

My sixth sense kicked in and I told the taxi driver to stop, otherwise I would open the door and jump out.

When the taxi driver stopped, I walked away, but K.S.'s brother followed me. We finally got to a restaurant, sat down, and I told him point blank that I was not interested in him.

"I am going to marry Kyung Ok's brother," I said that to make him back off and know that I was seriously not interested in him. I had no idea Hyung Lee (Ok's brother) would end up being my husband. God works in mysterious ways!

My Golden Wave

To make sure K.S.'s brother did not follow me to see where my home was, I told him I was going to the convent to see the nuns and I did not want him to follow me. Even after all that, he still sent me a blood letter forcing himself into my heart.

Like all my other friends, when I first met K.S.'s brother (because he was a jewelry maker) he gave me a green stone ring, but it was too big, it fell off my finger and disappeared. Thank God! That was another sign he was not meant for me.

Love cannot be forced no matter what. I taught that concept to myself from an early age and refused to go where my heart was not.

Effort to Build My Career

My Golden Wave

Academically, my first two years in Nursing School were a big struggle. I failed some subjects. My brain was going against what it was wired for; I loved and understood the arts very well, but not the sciences. The adjustment took a while.

On top of the academic struggle, I am not a night person. It was hard when I had to stay up to do the night shifts. But I trusted God knew where He was leading me, because on my own there was no way I could manage.

Fortunately, in the third year, the school took my class to learn by seeing, hearing and touching patients at the hospital. This was easier for me because I love to help people.

After seeing a patient in hospital, I returned to my room and studied the disease she or he had and how I could help her or him get better. That effort pushed me ahead. In clinical care, I graduated on top of my class.

I was expected to work in ICU (Intensive Care Unit) or the VIP unit, but instead, I chose to go to the Orthopedic Unit (Bone Unit).

My teachers and friends were surprised to see me choose the Orthopedic Unit. Deep in my heart, that is what I wanted to do. I got a job before I even graduated and started working as soon as I finished school.

Marriage

My Golden Wave

As I got closer to graduation from the Nursing School, Kyung Ok (one of my friends, also abbreviated as K.O. in this story), showed me a picture of her brother. And while in Korea, K.O. and her Mother created opportunities for me to meet him — at home and at his job site — but it never happened.

Another chance that K.O. thought would be great was when her brother was moving to the U.S.A. She and her mother arranged for me to meet him at the airport, but still, it did not happen. The flight was changed, and I missed it.

K.O. then asked me if I would be willing to go to the U.S.A and see whether I might like her brother. I never really entertained that idea. First, the U.S.A was extremely far, and secondly, I had no relatives or any friends there.

After graduation, my friend K.O. left for the U.S.A to join the rest of her family and to work. Among the things she took was my picture to her brother.

As a farewell gift I gave her the other of my 18-carat gold ring my mother had given me. Later, she gave it to my husband to measure the size of my finger when time came to buy my wedding ring.

It might have been my friend's mother who later became my mother-in-law that told her son to write me a letter. When I saw his picture again, I thought he was too old for me. But my father, I think liked him and told me not to judge by the picture.

Afterwards my family received a phone call from Hyung Lee in the U.S.A saying he was coming to see me. I told him not to come if he was only coming to see me.

But I think my mother-in-law told her son to persist and try to meet me, and if he did not like me, to just return home. So, when Hyung Lee came to South Korea at that time, he came straight to my home.

As soon as he saw my parents, he asked for permission to marry me. My father, even though he was not against the idea, said it was too soon. He suggested we try to at least know each other for a week.

Hyung Lee arrived in Korea on the 5th of December 1976, and on the 9th of December, we were legally married because papers had to be processed quickly for me to join him in the U.S.A.

My mother was so shocked. She cried so much because she felt she was going to lose her older daughter to a faraway country where she knew nobody.

When I saw my mother crying so much, I told her I would not get married, only the paper had been signed. It had no meaning (so I thought) because I was still a virgin. That consoled her.

Seeing what the situation was, Hyung Lee decided to go and visit another family member and later return to the U.S. A. alone.

During that time, my father asked an elder in his extended family to intervene. He also called Hyung Lee's older brother to help answer all the questions my parents had. They wanted to know more about my husband's family.

Before Hyung Lee returned to the U.S.A, the elders convinced my mother to let me be his wife. She eventually accepted, but still with a lot of tears.

My Golden Wave

We had a big wedding at Myung Dong Cathedral on December 28th, 1976. My husband gave me a diamond ring he had bought with the help of my sister-in-law to measure my finger. One of my 18-carat rings I gave to the Lord on my Confirmation day was returned to me with a diamond ring on my wedding day. That is how I looked at it.

The wedding was followed by a three-day honeymoon and then my husband returned to the U.S.A., to finish school and to work as he waited for me to join him.

My Golden Wave

Myung Dong Cathedral

My Golden Wave

Our Wedding Day

Arriving in the U.S.A

My Golden Wave

Processing my visa took seven months. My husband suggested that I stop working as a nurse and study English, so that it could be easier when I got to the U.S.A. to pass the exams, get a license, and start working.

In July 1977, the petition to join my husband was accepted and I received a visa to travel to the U.S. A.

My mother was very saddened because that same year my first brother left home to join the army for a mandatory service that was required of boys in South Korea. It was too much for her.

My father did not say anything, he kept everything in his heart, but I know he was worried too.

When I arrived in the U.S.A, I enrolled right away for English classes (ESL).

Even though I had been working hard and reading a lot of English books in South Korea, I still had a long way to go as far as mastering spoken-interactive English was concerned. At the same time, I had to study and pass the nursing exams to be certified to work as a nurse in the U.S.A.

My husband used to drop me off at the Northeastern University Library in Chicago in the morning and pick me up in the evening. I memorized a lot of material (medical books are so extensive). By the time I got home my head was so full and bubbling.

Luckily, I passed all the exams at the first take, even though for some subjects I was only on the borderline. I was -

My Golden Wave

simply happy for all the miracles that happened at that time.

After passing all the required exams, the toughest task of finding a job followed. I applied to many hospitals, but none of them could offer me a job. I was rejected from hospital to hospital. They were asking for experience. I wondered how one gains experience unless she or he is given a chance to gain it. I realized the American way was so different.

Finally, I got a job at the Thorek Hospital where my sister-in-law was working as a head nurse. That was another lesson to learn in America. To get somewhere depends on who you know. I mean, most of the time.

I started working at Thorek Hospital in the Medical Surgical Unit in 1978. I was overjoyed to have a job.

One day, after six months on the job, when I felt I was about to learn how things go in the Medical Surgical Unit, I was put to a test. The head nurse, the charge nurse and another senior nurse called in sick. I was still struggling to master the English Language when suddenly I became the charge nurse for that day.

To avoid any mistakes, when the doctor called, both the unit secretary and I picked the phone at the same time and listened in, to make sure I followed the right orders.

Another incident at my unit was about an expensive needle I cut. We used to cut used needles so they could not be picked from the trash and used for drugs on the streets. But the spinal taping needles were too expensive, so they were sterilized and reused. I did not know that. But seeing it was different from the others, I asked the charge nurse

My Golden Wave

and the senior nurse to be sure before I cut it. They both said it was okay to cut it, then I cut it.

The next day when the head nurse asked where the spinal taping needle was, I told her I cut it and threw it away. The charge nurse and the senior nurse never came out to say that they told me to cut it. I was surprised, but I kept that in my heart.

Pregnant with My First Child

My Golden Wave

In 1978, I got pregnant with my first-born child, Joseph, and gave birth in 1979. I was happy to become a mother and to get two months' maternity leave. I needed that time to catch up with my life.

After maternity leave, I took a new step and transferred to Weiss Memorial Hospital. But as I had no ICU experience, I was asked whether I was willing to take care of the dying patients. That was a big challenge.

To look at someone getting to the end of his or her life and seeing him or her take the last breath is an experience that stays with you for a while. And making sure a person is comfortable to the end is very demanding.

The only thing that made life bearable during that experience were my coworkers; everybody was truly kind, respectful, and loving. Without everybody's support, I am not sure I would have managed.

In 1980, I got pregnant with my second child, Justin, and gave birth in 1981. I was given two months again to stay home with my babies.

When I went back to work, my mother-in-law and father-in-law played a big role in taking care of my children as my husband was working too.

Eventually I changed my shift to night, to have more time with my babies during the day when they were awake. I did not want them to grow up without knowing who their mother really was.

That was a very trying time. At first, I was happy, I thought I would get time to be with my children. But to

My Golden Wave

adjust my brain to working at night and still being able to be with my children when I came home was as hard as *writing on water*.

Most of the time I came home very, very exhausted. I just wanted to sleep. Night shift was killing me slowly but surely, draining every ounce of energy from my body.

Some nurses used to take a fifteen-minute nap, which sometimes turned into an hour or more— when the patients fell asleep. I never took a nap because I was trained to never sleep on the job. I felt I had to be there all the time for the patients when I was on duty.

I am very thankful for my children; they were good to me. It was like they understood what I was going through.

When Justin woke up and saw me still sleeping, he stayed in his crib and watched me until I woke up. He never cried to wake me up. When I woke up and saw him right there, I thanked God he did not get ideas to wander away. Sometimes he laughed at me. I think he was wondering what was wrong with me!

Sometimes I slept in the doorway to prevent my children from running out of the house and maybe get hurt.

Taking my first child, Joseph, to day-care which was two blocks away, added to the struggle; coming home after a sleepless night, then feeding the children, taking one to day-care at 9:00 A.M (for three hours only), coming back home and resting for just two and a half hours, then going back to pick him up was a tough schedule.

My Golden Wave

In addition to the above, I was learning how to drive, which was a necessity to make life easier. But all that was seriously killing me.

I used to set an alarm to wake me up to pick up Joseph from day-care on time. Those who never picked up their children on time were penalized. But mainly, I did not want my child to wait at school when everybody was already picked up.

When the alarm went off, I was like a zombie, wondering, was it for picking up Joseph or taking him to school! Was it a phone ringing or what was it? That is how disoriented I was.

When my father-in-law died in 1984, I did not want my mother-in-law to be overburdened with my babies. So, I decided to handle everything by myself. I knew without any help, life was going to be overly complicated, and it was. I became extremely fatigued.

After realizing there was no way I could handle working full time and manage being a full-time mother as well, I told my husband that I was going to start working part time. He did not understand it at first. He said: "You want to buy a car and a house, then you want to work part time?"

I continued to work night shift but eventually fell sick. When I went to the doctor, he said there was a little problem with my liver. He also added that even if I reduced the work it would not change anything. He said I could seek a second opinion if I wanted.

I was not dead yet, but I knew I would be soon if I kept going the way I was going.

My Golden Wave

I used to go to Church occasionally during the week when I got a chance, but I could not go anymore because I was dead tired. I prayed so much for God's will to be done, for I had no control over what was going on in my life at that time.

I remember begging God for life, to live until my children grew up and be able to take care of themselves.

Even though I am not the best mother, I know for sure that for a child to grow up with a biological mother is better than a stepmother in many ways.

"Please Lord, let me live a little longer for my children," I prayed over and over.

I was not so worried about my husband because he could remarry, but life would be different for my children with a stepmother.

The next day after beseeching the Lord for mercy, a miracle happened. My husband asked: "Do you want to work part time?"

"Yes, even if it just one day a week less," I said.

"One day will be like full time. Why don't you take two days off and work three days a week?" He said.

He calculated the money that would be coming in and said that we would still survive with me working part time.

I call it a miracle because I had earnestly prayed to God for help. My husband did not know I was praying and seeking God's intervention. I will forever be thankful my prayer was heard, and my husband's heart was finally opened to respond positively to my plea.

My Golden Wave

When I got the chance to work part time, I treasured every minute of the days I stayed home with my children. Even though the workload at home was heavy too, I did not regret it. I balanced it with the joy of knowing that my children were growing up with their mother around.

How My Family Survived in America with Little

My Golden Wave

Once I changed to working part time, we did not have any savings to hold onto. And as a part timer, I was not covered by my work health insurance. We struggled a lot to raise our children. The fact that everything for children from diapers to shoes is expensive and outgrown fast, makes the struggle to raise children harder.

My two boys were growing so fast, sometimes the new school shoes I bought for them, hardly lasted 6 months. When I saw holes in them, I sewed them, but I knew their toes would hurt. I just wanted to delay buying new ones until a little later. Both boys grew up to 6 feet tall, though my husband is 5'7 and I am only 5'2.

When I went to buy groceries or anything, I looked for the cheapest I could find. I felt like it was written on the back of my head that I did not have much money.

I became very anxious about how our future was going to be, especially how we would be paying the bills without enough money. When you are in that state, sometimes you forget that even if you worry so much, only God has the power to change your situation.

One day, I opened my Bible and landed on Matthew 6:24:

> No one can serve two masters. He will either
> hate one or love the other. You cannot serve both
> God and mammon.

After I read it, I started to calm down. I kept that scripture open so that every time I became anxious, I could go back to it and reflect. It was a good feeling to be calm and let God take care of everything.

My Golden Wave

After a discussion with my husband, I took over writing the bills. When any bill came, I wrote the check and placed it in an envelope, and then wrote the mailing date with a pencil on it. When my paycheck and his paycheck came, I mailed them out one by one according to the date on the envelope. That way, we never missed a bill or paid late. God is so great. He took control of our situation from that time on.

(Mathew 6:25-27)

> [25] "Therefore I tell you, do not worry about your life, what you will eat or drink; or about your body, what you will wear. Is not life more than food, and the body more than clothes? [26] Look at the birds of the air; they do not sow or reap or store away in barns, and yet your heavenly Father feeds them. Are you not much more valuable than they? [27] Can any one of you by worrying add a single hour to your life?

Losing One of My Babies

My Golden Wave

As soon as Justin was born, I inserted IUD (intrauterine device) to prevent unexpected pregnancy. I knew that was against my belief, but I felt I did not have any choice. I thought I believed in God, but I did not put my whole trust in Him. I did everything my way.

One year after Justin was born, I found out I was pregnant again. I was surprised! I went into a panicky mode. I could not imagine how we could survive in America with three children. I told my husband that I was going to abort the baby. And I also asked my relatives what to do.

My husband did not totally agree to abortion, he left everything to me to make the decision.

One of my relatives asked: "This day, who is having three babies?"

The other relative said: "If you are already pregnant how can you abort the baby?"

I got very stressed and confused. I prayed hard, asking God to help me make the right decision. I was at the crossroads thinking, the more I waited, the older the baby grew.

Thinking deeply about the situation of my struggling family, I talked to my gynecologist to help me terminate the pregnancy.

That is something that later came back to haunt me for a long, long time even though I went for confession and I was forgiven. I never mentioned it again to anyone, but still thought about what I had done for many years.

My Golden Wave

Thoughts of my aborted baby came back especially when I saw a beautiful little girl at my church. Her mother did not terminate her pregnancy despite the intrauterine device she had in her womb that did work. I felt ashamed of myself and sad.

The truth is, I believed God had forgiven me. But I did not know I had not forgiven myself, until one day a famous speaker called Irene George from Ireland came to speak at our Church.

The topic was about healing. Among the many stories she shared, there was one that was exactly like mine. She said that there was a lady who had an abortion. She went for confession and God forgave her, but she did not forgive herself.

Those words went deep in my heart. I realized I had not forgiven myself; there was a bleeding wound deep down in my heart. I started crying. I did not even feel ashamed to cry out loud.

I believe through Irene God wanted to heal me so I could not suffer all my life. I was so thankful for God's mercy that healed me.

Since then, I got the courage to talk about the burden I had carried alone for many years because I felt healed. After that day, I decided to share my experience whenever I got a chance, to help other women who might find themselves in a situation like mine. I have shared it in this book for that same reason.

Becoming Pro-life

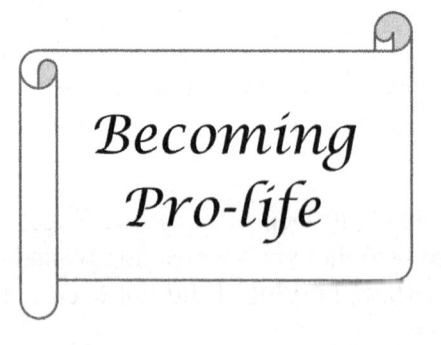

My Golden Wave

From January 20th to January 24th, 2004, I travelled to Washington DC with the Chicago Pro-Life Group for the Annual Pro-Life Procession.

The procession was about the 1973 case of Roe v. Wade, a landmark legal decision issued on January 22, 1973, in which the Supreme Court struck down a Texas statute banning abortion, effectively legalizing the procedure across the United States. Since the 1973 ruling, many states have imposed restrictions on abortion.

We arrived in Washington D.C on the 21st (the next day) and went to the National Basilica of the Immaculate Conception.

We sat for four hours in the Church waiting for Mass to begin. We had to be there early to get seats. The Church was filled by some activists, priests, cardinals, and many pro-life supporters like me.

Some children slept in the basement of the church because it was hard to find an inexpensive place to stay and rise early enough to attend Mass.

After Mass, we marched to the Supreme Court. It was a very overwhelming experience to see people from all over the United States fighting for the unborn.

After Mass, we had lunch (the Chicago group) with Cardinal George, simple lunch of sandwiches from the corner bakery.

My Golden Wave

Chicago Pro-Life Group in Washington D.C.

Right after I came back from that trip, I was put to a test. My good friend called me and told me she thought her daughter was pregnant and might not be able to take care of the baby. So, she wanted me to help her abort the baby.

I bought the pregnant test strips to go and test the girl to make sure she was pregnant.

When I got to my friend's home and saw her daughter's abdomen very round, I knew right away she was pregnant, but I tested her anyway to be sure.

My friend insisted she needed her daughter to abort the baby. She said that until it happened to her child, she thought she was pro-life, but she was not. She got very furious when I did not agree to participate in aborting the baby.

My Golden Wave

When my friend's daughter went to see the doctor, the doctor found out that she was six months pregnant, so, he could not help her abort the baby; it was not allowed.

My friend opted for adoption, and after all the screening they chose a family to adopt the baby.

The girl gave birth to a beautiful son. And I saw her expressing to her mother she wanted to keep her baby, and the baby was staring right into her face.

At that time, babies for adoption remained in hospital when the mothers were discharged. The hospital did not give away the babies right away just in case the mothers changed their minds.

When my friend saw her daughter sad and depressed, she changed her mind and allowed her to take the baby home.

The young mother worked hard to raise her son. He is now in high school and his mother is immensely proud of him.

I was so happy; I made the right decision on that one.

Teaching Catechism

My Golden Wave

In 1984, the Korean Church in Chicago was in its infancy stage and there was a need of someone to teach Catechism to the children.

One of my friends told the congregation that Mee Sook Lee was a catechist in Korea. When the priest asked me, I said yes, I could help, even though my schedule was very tight with my children still so small.

I worked night shift on Friday, Saturday, and Sunday. And on Sunday morning, I went to Church to teach the children. I was happy with the children, but when I came home, I felt like a dead body.

Eventually, my work changed again, and I became a registry; the hospital called me whenever they needed someone. Even though the pay was high, it was very unstable. On top of that, I still had no insurance at work and my family was struggling to survive.

Two years later my husband applied for a job in the City of Chicago as an engineer, but the pay was lower than the company he had been working for before.

My income and his income were low. We had a house to pay for and two kids to take care of.

I worked everywhere I was called to work: ICU, Cardiac Care Unit (CCU), and even in the Emergency Room, to raise enough money for our children to have a good education and pay the bills.

Despite our situation, sometimes I rejoiced when I was scheduled to work, and the following morning the numbers of patients went down, and I was told not to go. I used to:

My Golden Wave

"Thank you God!"

That made my husband so angry. But anyway, I was the only one who knew what my body needed. When it needed a rest and God gave it to me, I appreciated it.

Every time I went to work thinking in terms of money, I fell sick, but when I went to work just thinking about helping patients, I had better days.

In 1987, I stopped teaching Catechism to the children at my Church. Many things had changed. The Community wanted to do things a certain way. They also wanted to copy what other churches were doing.

When I was teaching everybody appreciated me because I did not only teach, I also watched their children while they were at Church. But when they felt they needed to change the Program, I felt I would not have much to offer.

The priest was disappointed and upset, but as I was the only one who knew what I could and could not do, I insisted that I stop.

I reflected a lot and realized that what was going on in my life was not what was bringing me happiness. I was famous at Church. Even my husband was called after me instead of the other way around; they called him Julia's husband.

When I put the Program together, I felt so good inside, but forgot to humble my heart and realize that God was the one working through me. I thought I was great.

Most of the time when I prepared lessons that I thought were wonderful and forgot to humble myself before God, the children never listened.

My Golden Wave

When I reflected on St. Bernadette's life, where she compared herself to a broom that was supposed to be used by Jesus and then put back in a corner. I felt I needed to change.

My ego was not letting me be a broom, used and put in a corner by Jesus, but I could not stop it. Therefore, to stop teaching was the best alternative; it could let other people use their creativity too for the good of the Church.

When I explained everything to the priest, and he understood. I was so happy.

Visiting My Mother

My Golden Wave

I made my first visit back home to South Korea five years after I arrived in the U.S.A, at my brother Jong Sun's wedding. My mother was in good health and we had some precious time together.

A few years later she got sick and my family thought it was a brain tumor; she was having seizures and passing out. When she went to hospital, they found out she had fluid in her brain. They did a procedure that helped her a little bit.

One time, my father called me to go to Korea to visit my mother because she was crying and asking to see me every time she got sick.

My father did not want me to know about the sickness, because of my family in the U.S.A. He thought I was busy with my children; he did not want me to worry. But he called because he did not want to regret it later after my mother died without seeing me.

When I went to see my mother in hospital, she was glad. She said she was also happy because she had seen Jesus in a dream. She said she was always afraid to die, but Jesus had showed her the joy of Heaven. She was not afraid anymore. She was telling everybody to believe in Jesus Christ.

When I first left for the U.S.A, my mother used to cry all the time because I was too far away, she could not see me. I was my mother's best friend, a daughter she was so proud of. At that time visiting or calling was awfully expensive. But every time I wrote to her, I told her not to worry about me, but to believe in Jesus Christ. And when that miracle happened, she was delighted.

My Golden Wave

That delight came from an experience. When my mother went to the Church I used to attend while in Korea (Catholic Church) nobody welcomed or greeted her. She stopped going there, wondering what kind of people those were.

As she continued to pass out, a protestant lady from the neighborhood approached her and told her about Jesus Christ. She taught her how to read the Bible. So, she decided to join the Protestant Church. People at that Church were so loving and welcoming.

After knowing Jesus, she stopped crying. Every time I called her, she praised Jesus, and was happy to hear her daughter's voice. I felt she was in good health. But when I talked to my father; he said my mother was still passing out.

When I visited my parents for three weeks, my mother did not pass out and I thought she was getting well. Unfortunately, that was the last time I saw her. I am glad I spent some quality time with her during that visit. I never visited any other friends in Korea, I paid my full attention to her.

Four years later, on the 17th of February 1989, my mother died in her sleep.

I wanted to be there for her funeral, but by the time I finished processing the visa and the ticket, the funeral was over.

I went home and stayed with my father for two weeks. He was incredibly sad and crying, blaming himself that he did not open the airway when my mother got a seizure because he was drunk that night. He had a tongue blade for opening the airway but did not use it.

My Golden Wave

I consoled him and thanked him for taking care of my mother throughout her sickness.

As we talked, I advised him to marry again. My two brothers did not agree to my suggestion. But when I asked them whether they were going to live with our father and take care of him, they did not answer.

I knew my father would be so lonely and unable to take care of himself. He could not cook or clean. My mother cooked and cleaned until she died despite her sickness.

Later, my mother's best friend introduced a lady to my father, and they married at the end of the same year my mother died.

I am so happy my stepmother was a very good-hearted person. She helped my father, visited my sister in the mental hospital and my brother when he was in jail.

My Brother Jong Sun

My Golden Wave

Jong Sun was two years younger than me. I remember when he was young, he fell sick often. He could get diarrhea and frequent abscess formations on his skin. But as he grew older, he became healthy. He was also a gentle person.

He attended *Shung In* Primary School like me and went to *Chung Woon* middle school and *Yongsan* High School. From high school I noticed he had built confidence in himself. He was able to go to Korea University and graduated from the Electrical Engineering Program.

Even before graduation, my brother was scouted to work with Samsung Company.

He worked hard, and in all things, he was guided by God who he worshiped wholeheartedly. His faith was influenced by his wife Sin Ja. They belonged to the Protestant Church.

For his work, he made overseas trips frequently. Unfortunately, those trips made him very exhausted.

One day, through the company checkup he was discovered to have an elevated liver enzyme. He seemed to overcome it well through good diet with the help of his wife.

I advised him not to make himself very tired if possible and to stop working for a while, but he said: "I love my work, it is okay." And continued working while having a physical checkup every six months.

In 1999, he had two overseas trips back-to-back and got so tired. When he went for checkup, they found he had a small tumor in his liver. He had surgery followed by chemotherapy.

My Golden Wave

On Sunday, January 16th, 2000, I went to Korea to see him. He was at home, not working anymore. We spent some time together and visited my sister in the mental institute. My brother hardly visited her because he was always busy. We were able to get new eyeglasses for my sister and she was happy.

We had a family meal which we had not had in a long time. My younger brother was the only one who was not there; he had had so many problems and was now living in an animal place, selling puppies. Jong Sun took me to see him. He could do that because he now had the time.

While I was still in Korea, during that same visit my brother Jong Sun was hospitalized again to undergo chemotherapy.

On the day I left to return to the U.S.A, he was discharged, and he came to the airport to bid me farewell. That was the last time I saw him.

He was hospitalized many times and received all the treatment that was available, but he eventually went under hospice care.

On the 11th of January 2001 during the morning Mass, I had a strong feeling to call my brother Jong Sun. When I called his home no one answered, so I called his wife's cell phone. She said that my brother had just died. I was very saddened.

I bought a ticket to go to Korea for his funeral, but by the time I arrived the funeral was over.

That first day I stayed with my young brother Jong Hwa. When I called my brother Jong Sun's wife, Sin Ja, and told

My Golden Wave

her that I was in Korea she told me to go to her home where she had lived with my brother.

Sin Ja had stayed with her parents because she was scared to go to her home after her husband's death. But now that I was there, she could return to her home with her two children: Min Woo and Hyun Woo.

That day was extremely cold, all the water pipes froze. We ate whatever was there until the water came back. We had time to talk and console each other.

Sin Ja told me about my brother's last days. All the family members said their last words to him. She also told me that my brother was very worried about his children who were still young. She told him not to worry about them, that she was going to take care of them. She encouraged him to be peaceful and submit to Jesus. And at that, he took his last breath.

A day later, Sin Ja decided to move closer to her son's school because he was a violin player. She had not been able to do that because she was taking care of her sick husband.

After breakfast, she called a realtor to sell her condominium. Few minutes later, the realtor called back and wanted to show the condominium to a buyer in two hours. We started cleaning right away. A friend from Sin Ja's Church walked in right on time. She was a great help since I did not know what to do and Sin Ja was very exhausted from her husband's funeral.

The condominium was sold on the first showing. Then the next task for Sin Ja was to find a place to live near her son's school. She called another realtor to help her find a house.

My Golden Wave

On the same day, in the evening we visited the house, and she made a contract.

That was amazing, she sold her house and bought a new one the same day! Selling houses does not happen like that in normal life. It was a miracle.

Sin Ja thanked God for letting that happen and for my being there for support. She said if I had not been there, she would have stayed with her parents for a while.

When I went to my father's home, I found my stepmother so depressed because of the death of her stepson. My father did not know what to do. So, I decided to take my stepmother out on a trip. When my nephew learned about it, he asked me to take his mother (Sin Ja) too.

So, we all went on a trip to Po Whang to visit my stepmother's daughter. We stayed in a hotel and we were able to rest. I was happy to see my stepmother smile when she saw her daughter and grandchildren.

I hold onto the Christmas and Happy New Year Card (below) which my brother drew in 1988 before he got sick. He drew it for my family. The picture shows me, my husband and my two boys. It helps me to keep his memory alive in my heart.

My Golden Wave

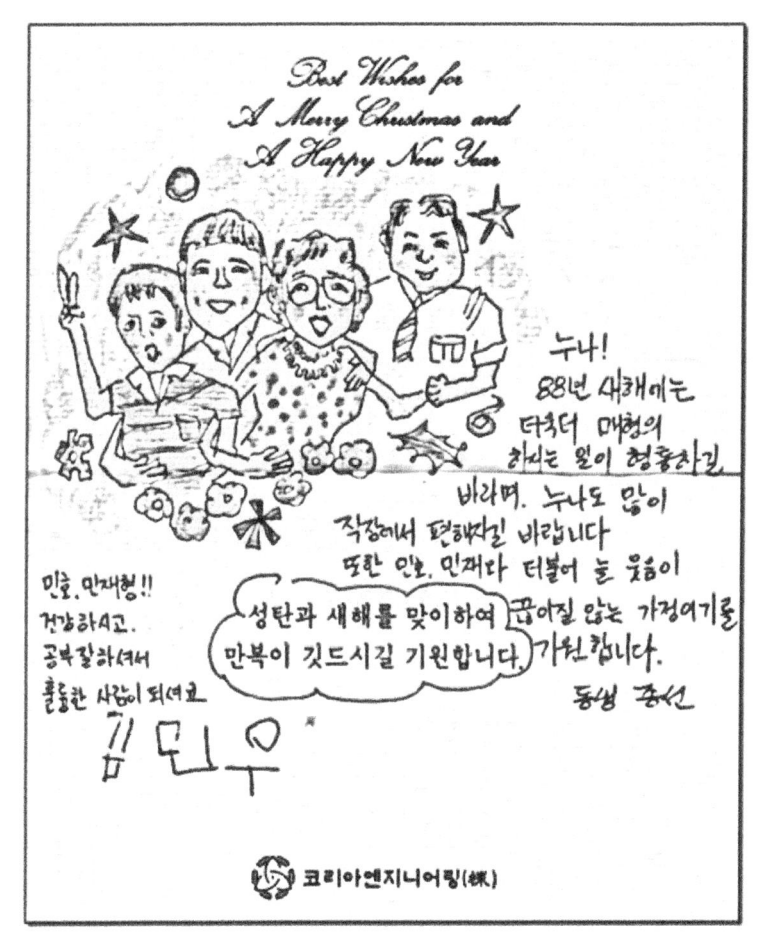

Picture of my family drawn by my brother Jong Sun

Closing of Ravenswood Hospital

My Golden Wave

In 1998 I was working at Ravenswood Hospital. I had worked there for 20 years, but the following incident caused that hospital to close, and I had to look for a job in another hospital.

The day the incident happened I was off duty; this is how it was reported by the Daily Press:

> Christopher (15) had been playing basketball with friends in an alley next to the hospital around 6 p.m. May 16. Suspected members of a Latino gang, who prosecutors say wanted to beat up an African American, approached the boys. One of them shot Christopher in the stomach.
>
> Christopher friends picked him, up, unconscious and bleeding, and carried him the 100 yards to the bottom of the ramp leading up to Ravenswood Hospital's emergency room.
>
> From where Christopher lay, according to reports, he was 35 feet from inside. Christopher's friends hustled inside the hospital to alert emergency staff.
>
> The chaotic events that happened next were Kafkaesque: Ravenswood policy dictated that emergency room workers could not go outside to treat patients...
>
> Christopher, with severe damage to his aorta, was pronounced dead at 7:33 p.m. A medical

examiner said he would have needed immediate surgery to repair his aorta...

The hospital was sued for 12.5 million by Christopher's parents for negligence.

Ravenswood Hospital was always on the news, even President Clinton talked about it.

In 1999, The Advocate Group bought Ravenswood Hospital. The salaries went up, and the benefits got better for some time. I was relieved that my job would continue.

But in the year 2000, the Advocate Group merged with Illinois Masonic Hospital. They took over the deficit of Masonic Hospital (which was too big). Then they realized they could not run both hospitals. So, they decided to close Ravenswood Hospital.

Ravenswood had Nursing, Nurse Anesthetic, and Radiology Programs, as well as Daycare and Alcoholic Recovery Programs. But the buyers had not paid attention. So, they could not keep everything going.

When they first announced that Ravenswood was going to close, they moved patient's schedules for open heart surgery to Illinois Masonic.

They closed each unit as soon as all patients were discharged or moved to other facilities. ER remained open until all units were closed. I was at the ER watching the Hospital lights go off one by one.

I told my husband that I was in a sinking boat and everyone was jumping off while I remained on it.

My Golden Wave

I did not feel like applying for a job at any other hospital at that time, after watching so many horrible things that had been done by the Advocate Group. I waited until the holidays were over to look for another hospital to work.

I took care of my last patient in ER at Ravenswood Hospital on Wednesday, June 20^{th,} 2001, but I remained in the hospital, even though there was no work for me. Sometimes there were only 10 to 15 patients a day.

To Holy Family Hospital

My Golden Wave

While I was waiting for the holidays to be over in 2001 and start looking for a job, my father and my stepmother from Korea visited me in Chicago. That was the first time any of my family members visited me. That was also the first time my parents and their in-laws met.

My father did not like the U.S.A., because of the communication barrier. He did not want to go out because if anyone said anything, he did not know what to say. But my stepmother loved it, she wanted to stay because "There was much cleaner air in the U.S.A," she said.

Together we traveled to Kentucky to see my stepmother's two sisters who were living there. My father and stepmother stayed in the U.S.A for two weeks. I was happy I was not working; I had some quality time with them.

When the new year started, I became nervous because I had to look for a job. I had never thought about looking for a job in my middle age. As an experienced nurse finding a job was not a problem but finding the right place for me was the issue.

I started praying, but I could not concentrate at home. So, I went to Church and sat down and prayed the rosary. As I prayed, Holy Family Hospital came to my mind. My former coworker had mentioned it to me before: "Come to Holy Family Hospital," she said.

I did not pay much attention then because it was eleven miles away from home. I thought it was too far.

I stood up and went back home, picked up my resume and went to Holy Family Hospital. I did not even check whether they needed nurses there, and I did not think about what department I wanted to work in. I just went.

When I walked into the hospital, I saw a sign reading: *Same Day Surgery*. As soon as I saw it, I thought, "that sounds good."

I went to the Chapel at Holy Family Hospital, and knelt and prayed: "Jesus, if you help me work here, whenever I come to this hospital, I will be coming in to say hello to you."

I filled out the application form and put Same Day Surgery and Telemetry as the Departments I wanted to work in, nothing else. But I was interviewed for the ER because that is where they were short of nurses.

It was not farfetched, I had it on my resume that I had worked in the ER before. I thought that is where the Lord wanted me to work.

They did not call me to work for more than a month. But one day, I received a phone call asking whether I was still available. I immediately said I was.

"Are you interested in Surgery Department?" The caller asked.

I laughed and said: "I have never worked in a Surgery Department."

"How about the PACU (Post Anesthesia Care Unit) and GI Lab (Gastrointestinal Lab) and Same Day Surgery?" The caller asked.

"Yes, I can work there," I said.

When the Surgery Department Manager interviewed me. He was delighted by my experience, and he suggested that I should work as a Registry Nurse instead of part-time as I had applied. I appreciated that because it was better for me at that time.

My Golden Wave

Registry is high fixed pay; I did not have to negotiate. And I could work in any department. The only bad side is that it has no health insurance or pensions.

I worked as a Registry Nurse in three departments as needed. I felt at home. I had never been happier. Coworkers were very friendly, and the patients were also patient. I felt it was a real holy family.

Two years later, I was shocked, the Administration started thinking about closing the hospital, due to financial problems. I was still recovering from Ravenswood Hospital closure. I could not believe what I was hearing.

I went to the Chapel and knelt and asked Jesus: "Why didn't you send me to Resurrection Hospital in Talcott instead of this poor place?" Talcott was close, only five miles from home.

When still at prayer, I felt like Jesus was asking me to read 1 Kings 17. I opened it and read it, and I was struck mainly by verse 16.

> For the jar of flour was not used up and the jug of oil did not run dry, in keeping with the word of the LORD spoken by Elijah.

Reflecting on that verse made me feel like they were not going to close the hospital. That maybe it was just a rumor. I continued to convince myself that it was not true.

But I was wrong. The process to close the hospital started and nurses were moving out and looking for other places to work.

I went back in the Chapel and knelt and said to Jesus: "See, the hospital is really closing."

Then I felt like Jesus was asking me to read the scripture beyond verse 17, that is 1 Kings 17:17-24. As I read it, I was struck by Elijah's prayer in verse 21:

> Then he stretched himself out on the boy three times and cried out to the LORD, "LORD my God, let this boy's life return to him!"

With the help of Elijah's prayer, I wrote my own for the hospital:

> "Oh lord my God, let this hospital return to life as a caring place."

Every time I went to work, I went to the Chapel and said that prayer.

The hospital departments started closing one by one, except the Surgery Department and the Key to Recovery Substance Abuse Center.

The name of the hospital changed to Resurrection Holy Family Hospital. A few months later, a Long-Term Acute Care Unit (LTAC) was established at Resurrection Holy Family Hospital.

It is now the only faith-based facility in Illinois. Right now, as I write this book, the hospital is open and surviving as AMITA Health Holy Family Medical Center. So, I am still working at the Surgery Department.

My Golden Wave

Celebrating my Birthday at Holy Family Surgery Department

My Golden Wave

At Holy Family Surgery Department

My Son Joseph

My Golden Wave

My son Joseph was born 1979. He was a careful and watchful boy. When he started talking, he was not talking much. He seemed confused by the languages we were speaking. For example, in English we say "snow" and in Korean we say *"noon"*, which is the same word in Korean meaning "eye". And a pear is called *bae*. That is the same word we use for "abdomen" and "boat."

One day I asked Joseph's teacher whether my son had a speech problem. The teacher said he had no problem. Later I realized he was confused by the languages we were speaking at home. I think he did not want to make a mistake; therefore, he did not speak much.

Joseph was wonderful child. When I vacuumed my house, he watched where I was going, and then pulled out the plug and plugged it in the room where he thought I was going to vacuum next. He always wanted to help in many ways.

When I brought groceries home, he watched where I put everything. The next time he helped me to put them where they were supposed to be. Sometimes he put them in wrong places, but he always tried to help.

Joseph attended Queen of All Saints Primary School in Chicago (a few blocks away from my home). He proceeded on to Loyola High School in Wilmette, a suburb of Chicago. And then went to the University of Illinois at Urbana-Champaign. He graduated with a Degree in Electrical Engineering in May 2001.

After graduation, he wanted to go to Korea to study Korean Language and History. He had gone to Korea twice for a short period when he was young and got interested in the culture.

My Golden Wave

One month after graduation, he left for Korea and joined Yonsei University's Korean Language Program. When the first three months expired, he extended his study twice, which ended up being nine months. After that, he returned to Chicago and tried to look for a job, but it was hard to find one.

When Pope John Paul II visited Canada for the World Youth Day in Toronto in 2002, Joseph went there with a Church friend. At the Mass Media Session, they learned that Mass Media was important in the world today. His friend got interested in filmmaking.

When they returned home, Joseph and his friend got busy making a documentary about their trip. It came out well, and they shared it with their friends.

Later, Joseph found a job and worked as a System Engineer in Chicago.

Later, Joseph's friend Kim, who was interested in filmmaking started making a documentary about *The House of Suh*, a tragic story described below:

> *The House of Suh.* One of Chicago's most famous murder cases surrounded sister and brother Catherine and Andrew Suh, first-generation Korean Americans, who conspired against, shot, and killed Catherine's former boyfriend. Over a decade later, director Iris Shim revisits the case and opens a Pandora's box of family secrets that reveals the murder to be anything but black and white. What emerges in *The House of Suh* is a riveting and tragic portrait of troubled family,

which shed light on the psychological complexity of cultural assimilation.

Kim thought Joseph would be good at editing the documentary, so, he invited him aboard.

Joseph was so happy to edit the documentary (more than doing his regular job, even though he still had to keep his job to have an income). Eventually, he quit his job and moved to New York in October 2008 to work with a film company.

The documentary titled *The House of Suh* was first released in 2010.

I visited Andrew Suh in Pontiac Correction Center on March 1, 2007 with my Pastor, Rev. Bang, and a friend. We went through heavy security check even though we had been cleared a month ahead.

Rev. Bang said that Andrew was in prison but was freer than him. He was very calm.

Andrew appreciated our visit so much and said that that was the first time a Catholic priest ever visited him.

Both Catherine and her brother Andrew are in prison for life. Andrew wrote the letter below to my husband:

My Golden Wave

이 선생님에게,

안녕하십니까?
폰티악 교도소 에있는 농쿨 안에서 인사를
보내드립니다.
이 편지가 너무 늦어서요, 죄송합니다.
17년 전에 이 선생님이 불상한 청소년을 길가에서
차지면서, 안전하게 집에 데려주셔요, 감사합니다!
제가 이 선생님이 내려주신 친절한 도움을 안 잊었습니다!
이 많은 시간에 지나가면서, 제가 선생님 다구 다시 영원히 언니는
언제는 이 선생님에게 아주 멋신는 아들 JOE 가 이 분쌍한
죄수 위해서 아주 큰 운동을 하려고있습니다!
제가 어른 축복을 받으면서요, 제가 서욱 영긴 희망을
남구었습니다!
제가 우리 하나님 아버지에게 많은 감사 기도를 드립니다!
이 간단한 편지를 쓰면서요, 너 이 선생님에게
감사드립니다.
몇년전에 이 청소년을 도와주시고 언제는 이 죄수를
안 잊어서낭!
이 선생님 과 너 동생 JOE 위해서 기도하구었습니다!

기도하는
서 승모
2007년
2월 5일

135

My Golden Wave

Translation of Andrew Suh's letter:

Dear Mr. Lee,

How are you sir! I am sending you greetings from a small cave at Pontiac Correction Center. I am deeply sorry for sending this letter so late.

17 years ago, you picked a poor boy from the street and took him home safely. Thank you so much!

Many years passed by, now I am connecting to you again. Your wonderful son JOE is a big support for this poor prisoner.

I know I am so blessed, and I have new hope. I am offering many thanksgiving prayers to God our Father.

I am ending this simple letter to Mr. Lee with many thanks for helping this boy many years ago and has not forgotten this prisoner. I will continue to pray for Mr. Lee and my brother JOE.

With Prayer Andrew Suh. Feb 5, 2007

My Golden Wave

Joseph lived in New York for three years. One day in August 2011, he invited us (his father and I) to visit him. When we went to New York, he took us on a tour. After the tour he disclosed his future to us. He said he wanted to go to South Korea and marry Jin sook.

Jin sook was a girl he had met in New York two years earlier. She had come to New York University for a master's degree. We first met Jin Sook when Joseph came home in Chicago with her during Christmas season in 2010, he introduced her to us.

She was very sharp and had good knowledge about Joseph's good and weak points. After she completed her master's degree, she returned to Korea where she had family and a job as a high school English teacher. She graduated on the top of her class in English. We are so proud of her.

When I asked Joseph whether he had already bought the ticket to go to South Korea, he said: "yes." And he was leaving in a month.

We were thinking they would return and live in the U.S.A after they married, but it was not going to be so.

History repeated itself, like my mother, I started crying over my son's decision to go so fa way. I cried a lone because I thought my husband would not understand.

Joseph came to our home in Chicago, and then left for Korea. After we returned from the airport, after bidding him farewell, my husband said that this was the first time he felt for my parents when he went to take me away from them. He said he felt a big hole in his heart. He cried.

137

My Golden Wave

"Thanks be to God; you finally understand my parents' pain," I said.

On December 18th, 2011, Joseph Married Jin Sook, we were happy to be able to attend the wedding. They now have a daughter Lauren Seol Lee.

Joseph is still working in the film industry. The documentary: *The House of Suh* attracted both my sons to start working in the film industry.

My Son Justin

My Golden Wave

My son Justin was born in 1981. As a child he was, and still is a very caring person.

At the time he was born, I was working the 3:00 P.M. to 11:00 P.M. shift. My husband took care of the boys when he came back from work between 5:00 P.M to 6:00 P.M. He fed them and put them to bed.

I used to come home around midnight. It was hard for me to wake up early in the morning to feed the children. Sometimes I slept in. Justin used to get up and play, and when he realized I was still sleeping he went back to sleep.

When I finally woke up, he woke up too and laughed so hard. Seeing me drowsy and trying to wake up, I think was funny for him.

Up to this day, I still wonder how a few months old baby, could be so patient and understanding! I felt sorry and guilty feeding him and changing his diapers late, but he never cried.

Like Joseph, Justin went to Queen of All Saints Grade School. He was active in sports, football, and Ice Hockey. He followed his brother to Loyola and Urbana, Champaign University and graduated with a Degree in Bioengineering.

After graduation, he studied for Real Estate license and became a Realtor. He followed his father who had a Real Estate Company and he worked under him.

In 2005, we bought a new house near our old house. Joseph and Justin lived in the old house, and later Joseph moved to New York. So, Justin lived in the three-bedroom house alone.

My Golden Wave

One day, I came home from work and found him baking a turkey in our new house. He was also cooking two other foods to go with the turkey. When I asked what the big meal was for, he told me it was for the homeless people.

He said that when he went to a shop to repair the car the previous day, a homeless person asked him for money. But he did not give him anything, and it was bothering him. Since he was also going through difficult time, he knew what it meant not to have what you need when you need it.

He put the food in brand new containers, and I went with him to deliver it to the homeless people.

When I asked him whether he knew where those poor people lived, he said: "yes." When we got there, I remained in the car while he delivered the food.

That was their only meal that day and they received it with gratitude. I was surprised none of them was even trying to get more to keep for the next day.

After we delivered the food, there were still a few containers of food left. We took them to my co-worker's home who was also in need of food. I had known her for a while, and I knew she was struggling to put food on the table, even though she had a job. She too appreciated very much.

In 2008, I met Y, my Korean Church member. When we had a chance to talk, I learned she was going through a difficult time with her husband. She was raising two daughters without getting his support.

My Golden Wave

As if that were not enough, her husband had sold the house on her, and she had been asked to move out by the buyer before the closing day.

Y did not want to move out because her younger daughter's graduation was going to be in five months. Therefore, she had to live within her school district.

My husband who was a realtor told her that she could not be forced to move out during wintertime. But in December 2009, she received a court order to move out of the house in six days. It was a few days before Christmas. For a court order you must obey, otherwise you go to jail.

When Y told me about the situation, I called all the people who could help. That evening, we met in Y's home with my husband, KO who was Y's boss, Justin (my son), and me, to find a solution.

Since there was no time to find a place to move to in just six days, Justin suggested that we should let Y move in his place. What a good heart!

We worked together to move Y; Justin arranged for the moving truck. I helped to clean Justin's home; KO helped Y to pack. We moved Justin's furniture to fit Y's furniture and her belongings in the house. Justin's friends he had been helping came in handy. They helped to lift the heavy stuff to where it was supposed to go. Y's place was twice Justin's place. So, there was no space left. Most of Justin's belongs were put in any place we found empty and in my house. He had a hard time finding his belongings later. Nine people and twenty of Justin's friends worked so hard those days.

Finally, we finished moving Y in three days before the court day. Everyone was dead tired, but happy for having made that miracle happen. It reminded me of "It's a wonderful life" in actor - James Stewart Movie.

We all worked hard, but everything fell in place mainly because of Justin and his friends.

Justin stayed with us for a short time and then moved to New York in January 2010. Joseph invited him to go and work with him. When Joseph was making a documentary of the *House of Suh*, Justin helped in some parts. Joseph introduced Justin to the film production work. It was hard for him to get into the industry as he had no experience; he struggled for a while, but gradually built up his career.

Andrew Suh, who is in prison changed my children's lives. They are both happy about what they are doing.

Justin married Jane Choi in 2014, and they have a son, Henry James Lee.

My Bother Jong Hwa

My Golden Wave

As I mentioned earlier, my brother Jong Hwa went as far as high school. He did not want to go to College. My mother advised him to go to a Veterinary School, but he refused. He just wanted to take care of dogs.

He raised a champion dog. When he traveled out of town, he took it to my mother and asked her to take care of it. He gave her instructions and asked her to make sure she put the vitamins in its food.

My mother complained to me often because my brother never bought vitamins for her. He only bought them for the dog.

Sometimes he was sent to jail when his dogs bit people and he could not pay for their treatment. My father bailed him out a couple of times. But once he realized my brother was not taking responsibility for his actions. He stopped bailing him out.

My father said that sometimes Jong Hwa was making good money, but he never told anyone because he was spending it on alcohol with his friends. My parents worried about him all the time.

One time, Jong Hwa was jailed for drunk driving. My mother died while he was in jail.

Later, my mother's worry became my stepmother's worry. Since my father did not bail him out anymore, my stepmother worried about him so much staying in jail. I sent some money to bail him out. Unfortunately, his heavy drinking continued.

One day he was caught drinking and driving during his suspended period. It was too expensive to bail him out -

because the posted bail was ten times higher, we could not afford it. So, he stayed in jail for a year. I was only able to send him a letter. My stepmother visited him in jail, but my father did not.

When he got out of jail, he was not allowed to drive anymore. That set him back a whole lot.

Jong Hwa eventually found a good girlfriend who helped him set up the dog business he wanted. She got to know him very well. She was the only one who understood his talent with dogs while everyone else was laughing at him and thinking of him as troublemaker.

My brother got his life together and even called me one time to say hello. That was very unusual; my family called when there was a need or a problem or sickness in the family. I was the one who always called to just say hello.

When I went to visit him, my brother introduced to me his girlfriend. She was gentle and nice. She was the best person he had ever met.

With her help, he bought land in a suburban area and started raising and training many dogs. He took me there to see his work. He seemed to have never been better and happier in his life.

In October 2008, one week after my pilgrimage to Medjugorje in Bosnia. I received a phone call from my sister-in-law Sin Ja (my first brother's wife) saying that my brother Jong Hwa was diagnosed with end-stage liver cancer. So, I packed my luggage again and headed to Korea.

My Golden Wave

I was worried I was going to find him gone. I prepared for the funeral — I took the dress and everything — and my husband gave me some extra money for the funeral.

When I got to Incheon, there was no one to pick me up from the Airport anymore. I took a bus to the hospital where my brother was. I was happy to find him alive, and surprisingly still in the Emergency Room.

Even though the family members now knew, nobody had told him he had liver cancer. I am the one who told him. The doctor advised him to go to another hospital for a liver transplant. But he said: "No, I will not face surgery, I will get better."

When I told the doctor that my brother did not want to have a liver transplant, he sent him to the ICU.

Since the hospital was far away from my father's home, I needed a place to sleep. Fortunately, there was a room in the basement of the hospital for families that had a patient in the ICU and had nowhere to stay. They accommodated me.

After I found where to sleep, I went to my father's home during the early hours of night, to see him before he went to slept.

Later, my stepmother and I took some blankets and went back to sleep at the hospital in the room they had given me. I woke up from time to time, I think due to time difference and worrying about my brother. I went to the Chapel and said the Rosary. We were all going through a hard time; my brother's girlfriend was crying, and my stepmother was depressed.

We stayed at the hospital the entire time, visiting my brother three times a day until he was transferred to the regular floor.

The reason I prepared myself for a possibility of a funeral, is because during my nursing career in Korea, I had seen patients with liver cancer brought to the ER and died within twenty-four hours. Most poor people go to hospital at the last hour.

Later I found out that at the time my brother went to hospital, five other people showed up with the same problem but did not survive. He is the only who survived to live a little longer. I heard that the reason he survived is because they found the bleeding point and closed it.

For Koreans, liver cancer is common. Doctors are always trying to figure out how to extend life, at least a little bit, for every liver cancer patient.

Sr. Caritas, who I had known very well from my Chicago Church, happened to be at the hospital where my brother was in Korea. She was now the head of the hospital nuns there. She asked whether my brother was willing to believe in Jesus Christ. And when he said yes, Sr. Caritas started teaching him Catechism.

After he was discharged, my brother continued to go for Catechism classes. He received Baptism from the hospital Chaplain in 2008. He became a member of the Neighborhood Church until he got sick again.

I stayed in touch with his girlfriend who was now taking care of him and the business. Sometimes my stepmother relieved her so she could get some rest.

My Golden Wave

At one point my brother's abdomen became so big the doctor had to tap the fluid to reduce it. But after removing the fluid, he got weaker and weaker. So, I decided to make another trip to Korea to help him. My husband was so upset I made the trip again.

When I got there my brother was lying flat on his bed. He could not open his eyes or lift a finger, but I knew he was hearing me. I told him I had gone back because of him.

When I checked his blood pressure and pulse, they were low but stable. His girlfriend and I decided to just sleep next to him and wait for what God had planned for him.

While we were sleeping, he coughed and woke us up. When I looked at him, he was vomiting. The vomit was coffee ground color, which meant he was bleeding from the stomach. I told his girlfriend to call an ambulance and she started crying.

My brother was taken to the Emergency Room. Surprisingly, the room was terribly busy and noisy, but they attended to him. They put a tube through his nose to the stomach and removed the same color fluid he had vomited. They gave him some medicine to raise his blood pressure because it was very low.

After he got stable, I checked to see where all the noise was coming from in the Emergency Room. That is when I realized most of the monitor wires of the patients were going off because they were restless. That is what was causing the noise. I started putting them in their right places because I believe a nurse is a nurse everywhere.

In the morning of June 21st, 2009, I called all the family members, to be there as the Chaplain gave my brother the last Sacraments.

My Golden Wave

My father asked my brother to forgive him his wrongs to him and my brother asked for the same. After everybody bid him farewell. He took his last breath surrounded by his family.

His church members came to the hospital to pray for him after he died. The trained Church members cleaned him and dressed him in a traditional cotton cloth. I was with my family watching and praying through the glass window.

They then placed him in a coffin to take him to the cremation place. They continued to pray for him during cremation.

I am forever thankful and pray for such kind people who took care of my brother and allowed us to grieve. They spent three days with us even though my brother attended that Church for just a short time. May God bless them.

Before returning to the U.S.A, I prepared a table with a prayer book, a crucifix and a candle and set them in my brother's room to help my brother's girlfriend pray and not be scared.

The Last Days of My Father

My Golden Wave

My stepmother was a blessing to my family because she was a kind and warm-hearted person. She looked at my brothers and sister as her own children.

She said that she was staying with the family not only because of my father, but because of the children. We all appreciated her.

My father got a chance to travel to the U.S.A with my stepmother which he never did with my mother because of her poor health.

Unfortunately, in April 2012, my father's health started to decline. The long history of high blood pressure and alcohol weakened his heart.

He was living on the 4th floor with no elevator and used to go early every morning to get spring water. But he could not do that anymore. He was in and out of the hospital and nursing home twice that year.

My father did not want to stay in the nursing home; he insisted he wanted to go back home. It was hard for my stepmother to take care of him; it was a full-time job.

After Thanksgiving of 2012, I went to Korea to take care of my father for three months: giving him a bath, checking his blood pressure and heart rate, and reporting back to the doctor to get medication for him.

My father said he wanted to die at home not in the hospital. He had a horrible experience every time he went to hospital. Due to alcohol withdrawal, he got confused and they used to tie him down. He hated that so much.

My Golden Wave

Three months elapsed without my father getting better. I knew my stepmother could not take care of him at home. I tried to convince him to at least go to the nursing home. But no matter how hard I tried; he did not want to. I told my stepmother that maybe my father would agree to go to hospital once he could not really breathe. I felt sorry for my stepmother.

A month later, after I returned to Chicago, he was hospitalized for the last time.

In the hospital, he received an emergency Baptism on March 5th, 2013 from a visiting Catholic Chaplain. On April 6th, 2013, he died.

His funeral (cremation) was conducted by my stepmother's Church which had its own funeral home. That was a blessing. We then placed his ashes in the Korean National Cemetery.

In 2014, I was able to place my mother's ashes next to my father's.

Taking My Sister Out of a Mental Institution

My Golden Wave

After my father's funeral, I returned home to Chicago in April 2013. But in my heart, I felt I needed to take my sister from the mental hospital. Every time I visited her, the doctor advised me to take her out, but she did not tell me there was a better place for her to be.

My father had paid the mental hospital to keep my sister for life, but the hospital wanted her to get out so they could admit another person who could pay more. Probably the payment my father paid ran out.

I had no power to take my sister out of the mental hospital when my father was still alive. But now that he was gone, I felt I needed to set her free. When the thought of taking her out came to me, I had to make sure she was willing to get out.

One day, I called my sister at the mental hospital to let her know that I wanted to take her out. I told her I did not know any place to take her yet, but I wanted to know whether she was willing to leave the mental institution to a rehabilitation place.

She listened attentively and said: "YES! If you take me out, I will be good." She was so happy.

I told my sister not to tell anybody yet because I did not know where to take her, but to quietly prepare herself.

I was not good at searching for anything on the internet then, but I tried and found one hundred and fifty different places in Seoul.

I started selecting those that were close to where my sister lived. I eliminated the women only, and the privately run facilities. She had lived in a mixed gender and government run large facility for thirty years. I wanted to find a similar place.

Once I had selected a few good places, I returned to Korea. My son Joseph had said he would have the time to drive me around, but when I got there, he was too busy to help except on weekends.

I took a bus and a train to visit the facilities I had selected. Then on weekends, Joseph and his wife, my sister and I, visited the facilities together. It was a tedious work, but we finally picked one.

On August 27th, 2013, I went to the mental hospital for my sister's discharge.

We walked out of the hospital with one carry-on and two backpacks. That was all my sister had as her belongings.

I asked her whether she was going to miss that place and she said: "Never, I will never come back here again."

My Golden Wave

My sister (left) and me (right) when I got her
out of the mental Hospital in September 2013

My Golden Wave

I stayed with my sister in my son's home for a while, and after I placed her in the new facility for six months.

The first two weeks at the new facility were for observation and evaluation. From there, she would either be sent back to the mental hospital or eventually find a new long-term rehabilitation place.

I extended my stay for two weeks until they fully accepted her. I was very thankful to God for that miracle.

She was so happy in the new place. She had freedom; she could go to the market and to Church because they were close by. The staff paid attention to her and liked her. They kept her for six months to adjust.

Six months later, I returned to Korea with my husband. As the first place was only for six months and for only those who had just been discharged from hospital. I had to search for a new, long term place.

Because my sister had done well for those six months, she could then go in a three-year program facility, but it was hard to find one in Seoul, we had to look outside the City.

Finally, I found a place near Seoul and I called them to find out whether they would accept my sister, at her age and condition. In that facility there were only twelve clients at the time out of a capacity of fifteen.

On the appointment day, my husband, my son Joseph, Jin Sook, and myself accompanied my sister to the new facility. They did a simple test and accepted her. She said she liked it. The staff was happy to see her.

After all those years in a mental institution and at her age she was answering the questions very well.

We decided to let her be admitted in that facility. Two months later, she took a plane trip with the other members at the facility to Jeju-Do, a small island south of Korea.

At first, she was so scared to go on a plane. She had severe motion sickness, but with medication she made it and enjoyed herself. She was proud of herself. That was the best time of her life. She engaged in a lot of activities.

My sister in Jeju Do

At the facility, she was good and obeying the facility rules, but gradually she became bossy and stopped listening to the staff and started going against the rules.

The following year when I visited her, I took her out to stay with me. The first thing she said was that she wanted to get married to a man she met at the facility.

My Golden Wave

I carefully explained to her that it was not possible unless I was in Korea to watch over her or if the man's parents agreed to look after them.

She got so mad; she did not want to stay with me anymore. She wanted to go back and stay with the man she wanted to marry.

The next day, I took her back to the facility, but her behavior worsened, she hardly listened to the staff.

In February 2017, at the end of the third year at the facility, they could not stand it anymore, they called me to take her out.

I arrived in Seoul on February $8^{th,}$ and the first thing I did was to go to her facility to get her. She was aggressive and angry with the staff and even with me. Because of her violent behavior, they wanted her out as soon as possible.

Since she refused to go to hospital, they advised me to take her to the doctor's office. The doctor advised hospitalization, but only parents had the power to allow hospitalization, and they were both dead.

The doctor prescribed a heavy dose medication for her. When we brought her home and gave her the medicine, she fell asleep after a short time.

After dinner, I gave her the second dose. An hour later she sat up and read a prayer book. But suddenly fell backwards and slept till the next morning. Luckily, she fell back on blankets, otherwise she would have injured her head.

Every time she woke up, she called the old and the new facilities. I told her I was going to take her phone to charge it, intending to take it away from her, but she did not forget about it. Later she said: "Give me back my phone, otherwise I won't like you."

After dinner, we gave her the medicine again. An hour later she fell asleep. I slept near her, checking on her throughout the night.

She laid down like a dead person. She had a weak pulse and never moved at all. For many hours, she never woke up. I woke up every now and then to move her arms and body for circulation. When she woke up later, she could not stand, she crawled and fell in the bathroom. Thankfully, she did not hurt herself.

I spoon-fed her while holding her on a chair, otherwise she fell back. When sitting on the couch, she just opened her mouth, fell back, and slept. She became normal after 4:00 P.M and then I gave her another dose as the doctor prescribed.

The next day, when I called the doctor and explained how my sisters was responding to the medicine, he said I could give her half a dose. With that adjustment, she did well. After that week of struggle, my sister became stable.

We then started heading to the new facility at Dae Jon, three hours away from Seoul where Jin Sook had found two facilities. We visited those places and decided on one where the staff seemed to be very experienced. They did not seem to be afraid to take her and if she needed admission, she could get it under the government approval. We placed her in that place.

Two months later, in a new facility my sister was admitted for a month in a mental hospital. All aggressive behavior stopped.

She did not remember much about the other facility after she was discharged from hospital. I do not know what kind of treatment she was given. Maybe she received electric shocks in the brain. But I am not sure, for they were not using that treatment often. It was only for chronically ill patients like my sister. I am thankful she got better.

Unfortunately, in 2019 she broke her ankle and ended up in a nursing home until she healed. She was readmitted in the facility and she will be there for three years.

In December 2019, I went to Korea to celebrate my sister's 60th Birthday.

My sister's 60th Birthday

My Golden Wave

My sister's 60th Birthday

On September 15^{th,} 2020, I received a phone call from Dae Jon facility saying my sister could not get out of bed in the morning. She was so weak but able to change her clothes by herself.

For the last three years she had been coughing on and off without any fever or change in lung x-ray. And she kept losing weight, even though she was eating well.

The case manager said she could not admit her to a hospital unless tested and had negative Covd. 19 results. Therefore, she took her to long term care hospital at Dae Jon City to be tested. The results came back negative and she was then admitted, to see what was going on.

I am thankful my son Joseph is there. He went to see her even though for a short while due to the pandemic. He also helped to do all the necessary paperwork for my sister to officially be discharged from the previous facility to a new long-term care hospital.

She is still weak and getting physical therapy. I am praying for Covd19 to subside so I may get a chance to visit my sister again.

My Health Scare

My Golden Wave

For the 2014 visit to Korea I had two missions: to move my sister to a new facility and to place my mother's ashes next to my father's ashes.

After taking my sister to a new facility, my daughter-in-law arranged for me to have a medical checkup in a hospital near her place. With $500 I could have blood work, ultrasound of abdomen and chest Xray and more. The procedure took four hours.

After the checkup I went to arrange for my mother's cremation. While doing that I received a phone call from my daughter-in-law. She said she had received a phone call from the hospital about the ultrasound. I had to return the next day for a CT scan.

The next day I saw a liver specialist. He showed me the picture of a 6.6 cm tumor in my liver. He suggested that if I had a liver transplant, I could live for four years more. "There was 90% of liver cancer," he said.

I thought he was 100% sure because of my family history and the size of the tumor. So, he sent me to the CT scan. As I walked out of her office, I prayed: "Oh Lord! Thank you and I praise you, the doctor said I have liver cancer. it is my turn now." That prayer helped me to calm down and fear disappeared. I remembered that prayer from Thessalonians: 5:16-18.

Everybody in my family who heard the news was shocked and scared about my health. My husband seemed to have a mental block. When he received a phone call from our friend who was watching our house in the USA that our roof was leaking from heavy snow, he could not even give the instructions to resolve the problem. So, I instructed our friend on what to do. I could do it because I was at peace.

My Golden Wave

I had the CT scan done and came home. I decided to think about my liver cancer later. I concentrated on finishing my mother's cremation.

We exhumed and moved my mother's body to place her in the coffin and transfer her to the cremation place. By the time we finished the cremation, the national cemetery was closed. So, I kept the ashes in my room until Monday when we were able to place them next to my father's ashes.

The next day I went to get the CT scan results. Good news, the doctor said I did not have liver cancer, but I had something in the small intestines. He advised me to check it out.

He said I should see an intestine specialist. CT scan showed a neuro-endocrine tumor.

In my heart I thought, if I have passed the liver cancer scare, what could be worse! Instead of having another test, I decided to have surgery and remove it.

After I scheduled surgery I came home and researched on Google what that tumor was, because I had never heard of it. It came up that Steve Jobs suffered from that kind of cancer and later it became pancreatic cancer.

On the 4th of March 2014, I had a small bowel resection and removed a 10cm small bowel. Post operation diagnosis was 1cm size of heterotopic pancreas. It was found out that one small pancreas cell had invaded the small intestine, but it was not cancerous, I did not need chemotherapy. "Thank you, God!" I said.

My Golden Wave

I was in hospital for one week, went home, and then returned after three days to have the stitches taken out.

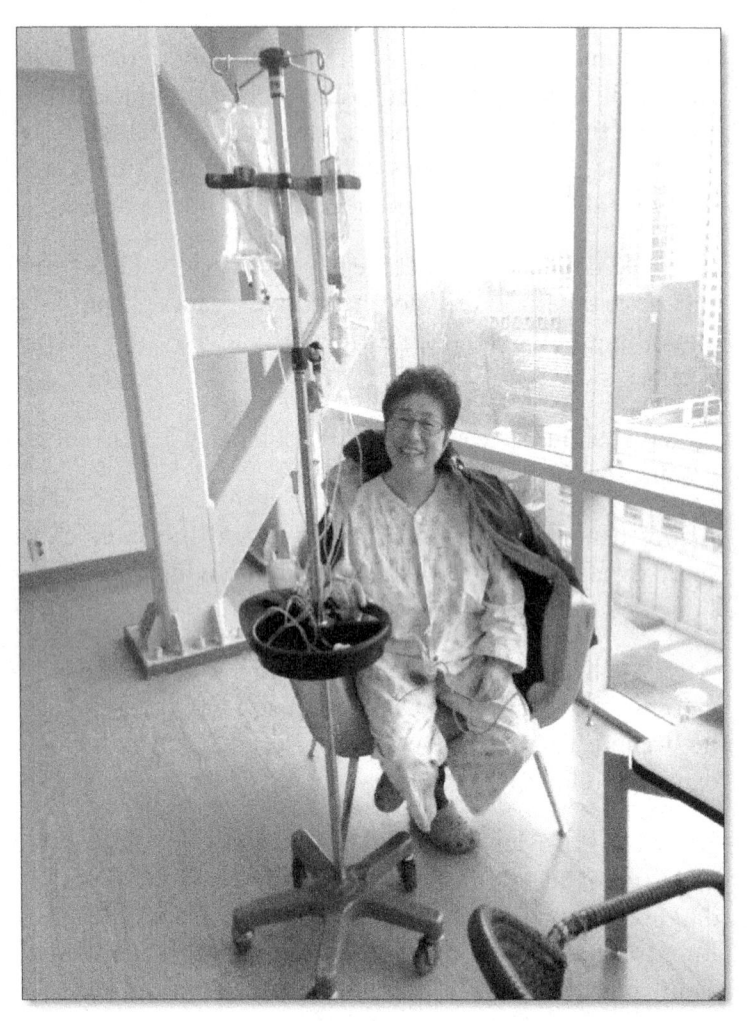

After surgery

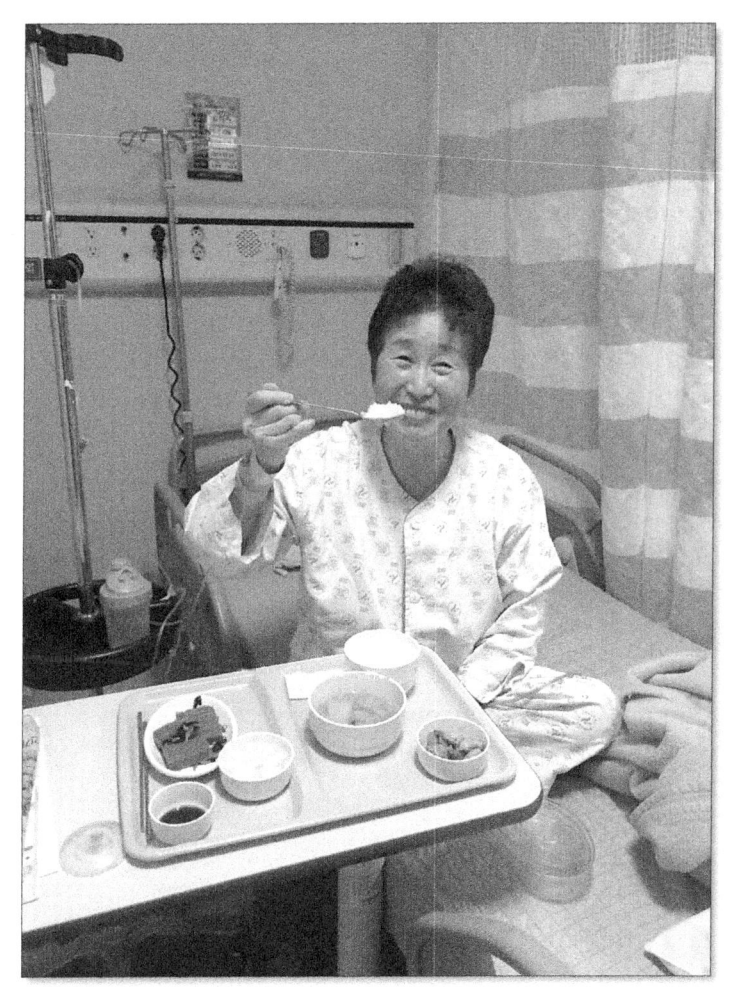

My Golden Wave

After surgery

My Golden Wave

On March 17th, 2014, I flew back home with an abdomen binder.

I was so glad to be back and attend Justin and Jane's wedding in New York on April 5, 2014.

I remember, I prayed desperately when I first got sick, that I may live a little longer for my children. I asked for about ten years more, so they could grow up and take care of themselves. I am thankful I have seen both grow up, get married and I have seen my grandchildren. My golden wave of life is continuing from children to grandchildren.

I feel blessed, God has been so loving and merciful to me. I will thank and praise Him forever.

I would like to end with the passage that I feel brings my life together.

I Thessalonians 5:16-18:

> Rejoice always, pray continually, give thanks in all circumstances; for this is God's will for you in Christ Jesus.

Messages from Friends

My Golden Wave

I have crossed path with many people at work, at Church and other places who became my extended family. I would like to humbly share (with permission) two of the notes I received from some of my friends when I told them I was writing a book.

A Kind and Loyal Friend

Claudia Kowal

I first met Mee Sook Lee back in April 2002 when she joined the registry nursing pool for Same Day Surgery at Holy Family Medical Center. My first impression of her was friendly, caring, and spiritual. It did not take long before I discovered what drew me to her and we became dear friends. The loyalty, sincerity, truth, and love inside her spilled onto me. Working with Mee Sook is always a pleasure. Her bubbly personality is hard to ignore. She is an excellent nurse.

She gives her all when taking care of patients with passion, love, and professionalism.

Mee Sook's kindness and generosity are the norm for her. She has this infectious smile and laugh with a positive attitude. I have been blessed to be a recipient of her friendship. Mee Sook is always willing to help, listen, and offer her thoughts as well as prayers in times of need for all.

My Golden Wave

Faith and family are her focus in life. Mee Sook wears a rosary bracelet as an everyday piece of jewelry. Prayers fill her daily life no matter what is going on.

When Mee Sook talks about her family, she has a sparkle in her eyes, and you can just feel the love she has for them in her heart and soul. Now that she is a grandmother, the family love seems even more intense with pride as she beams talking about the grandchildren.

Mee Sook is a very upbeat and optimistic person. She is a healer. When someone is hurting or going through a rough time Mee Sook opens her heart and offers prayers, time, support, and often financial generosity. As a friend, you can depend on Mee Sook to be there ready to give and she asks nothing in return. Mee Sook is a beautiful friend inside and out. Her heart is made of gold and she has the wings of an angel.

Everyone who comes into Mee Sook's life has a friend forever and a special spot in her heart. I have been so blessed to have her in my life as both a co-worker and dear friend and to know her kindness, compassion, and love.

My Golden Wave

The message below titled *"Meeting Mee Sook Lee"* is from Sr. Stella Sabina from Uganda.

Meeting Mee Sook Lee

Sr. Stella Sabina

In 2004, I moved to Indianapolis after exploring and realizing Washington D.C. was too fast and too expensive. Indianapolis' pace was slower and not as expensive.

As I knew nobody in Indianapolis, I started by making friends, for human connection and learning how life was in this new place.

Some of the friends I made took me on a trip to Chicago to attend a Charismatic Prayer Convention. There, I also got a chance to have a booth to sell my book, crafts, and other items for fundraising.

It was a very wonderful weekend, even though I was not able to attend all the sessions because I had to watch my table in the hallway.

Among the people who came by my table was Mee Sook Lee. She bought my book and talked to me for a while. She asked me why I had a smile on my face all the time.

"That is how God created me," I said.

My Golden Wave

The truth is, I did not come out of my mother's womb smiling. It is something I worked on daily, after getting tired of being angry about all the things that happened to me in the past. I was happy when someone noticed.

After that interaction, Mee Sook Lee and I became friends forever. Looking back now, I realize there is no way I would have survived everything I have survived without Mee Sook's help.

In 2006, when a friend who was helping me to sell my crafts to pay rent and to sustain the girls I sponsor in school was shot and killed in Indianapolis, Mee Sook Lee stepped in to help. She has been helping to fill up the balance of my rent almost every month for fourteen years to date. I had never seen such kindness in my life.

Mee Sook has a kind and simple heart that you cannot forget. Her joy is contagious! She always wants everybody to be okay, with a roof over her or his head. And not to go to bed on an empty stomach (Matthew 25:35).

I think God has a special place for Mee Sook in Heaven because her life is always answering the question, *What Would Jesus Do?* and follows Jesus' teaching.

I lift her every day in prayer that the Creator may bless her ever generous and loving heart. She is one of the kindest people I have ever met.

My Golden Wave

Sr. Stella and me in Indianapolis, 2019

Sr. Stella with her girls in Uganda

Sr. Stella (right) with her friend Mary (left)

Made in the USA
Monee, IL
12 November 2021